# 75 SIMPLE
# MIDDLE EASTERN
## RECIPES

### STEP BY STEP IN 250 PHOTOGRAPHS

SOHEILA KIMBERLEY

southwater

This edition is published by Southwater, an imprint of Anness Publishing Ltd, Hermes House,
88–89 Blackfriars Road, London SE1 8HA; tel. 020 7401 2077; fax 020 7633 9499
www.southwaterbooks.com; www.annesspublishing.com

If you like the images in this book and would like to investigate using them for publishing, promotions
or advertising, please visit our website www.practicalpictures.com for more information.

UK agent: The Manning Partnership Ltd; tel. 01225 478444; fax 01225 478440; sales@manning-partnership.co.uk
UK distributor: Grantham Book Services Ltd; tel. 01476 541080; fax 01476 541061; orders@gbs.tbs-ltd.co.uk
North American agent/distributor: National Book Network; tel. 301 459 3366; fax 301 429 5746; www.nbnbooks.com
Australian agent/distributor: Pan Macmillan Australia; tel. 1300 135 113; fax 1300 135 103; customer.service@macmillan.com.au
New Zealand agent/distributor: David Bateman Ltd; tel. (09) 415 7664; fax (09) 415 8892

**Publisher:** Joanna Lorenz
**Senior Cookery Editor:** Linda Fraser
**Copy Editor:** Christine Ingram
**Designer:** Siân Keogh
**Photography and styling:** Patrick McLeavey, assisted by Jo Brewer
**Food for Photography:** Jane Stevenson assisted by Jane Hartshorn
**Illustrator:** Madeleine David

### ETHICAL TRADING POLICY

Because of our ongoing ecological investment programme, you, as our customer, can have the pleasure and reassurance of
knowing that a tree is being cultivated on your behalf to naturally replace the materials used to make the book you are holding.
For further information about this scheme, go to www.annesspublishing.com/trees

Previously published as *Essential Middle Eastern Cooking*

### NOTES

Bracketed terms are intended for American readers.

For all recipes, quantities are given in both metric and imperial measures and, where appropriate, in standard cups and spoons.
Follow one set of measures, but not a mixture, because they are not interchangeable.

Standard spoon and cup measures are level. 1 tsp = 5ml, 1 tbsp = 15ml, 1 cup = 250ml/8fl oz.

Australian standard tablespoons are 20ml. Australian readers should use 3 tsp in place of 1 tbsp for measuring small quantities.
American pints are 16fl oz/2 cups. American readers should use 20fl oz/2.5 cups in place of
1 pint when measuring liquids.

Electric oven temperatures in this book are for conventional ovens. When using a fan oven, the temperature will
probably need to be reduced by about 10–20°C/20–40°F. Since ovens vary, you should check with your
manufacturer's instruction book for guidance.

Medium (US large) eggs are used unless otherwise stated.

Main front cover image shows Shish Kebab – for recipe, see page 34

*Pictures on pages 1, 7 and 8:* Zefa pictures

# CONTENTS

# INTRODUCTION

For over three thousand years the Middle East has been the crucible of many civilizations – the Babylonians, Armenians, Assyrians, Persians, Greeks and the Romans to name but a few – and in the process it has acquired a rich cosmopolitan character.

While most of us eat to live, the typical Middle Eastern person lives to eat. There is, however, more to it than that – food plays a very important social role. A Persian saying sums up the attitude to food perfectly: "*Mehman Hediyah Khodust*" (A guest is God's gift). And indeed there is no better way to look after a guest than to give him or her good food.

Such is the importance of a guest – whether he or she be a member of your own family, a friend or indeed a stranger – that when food is prepared an extra amount is always added, just on the off chance that someone may call by during the meal. At our home in Iran, for instance, we always kept open house on Fridays, the equivalent of Sundays in the West, and my mother made sure that plenty of food was prepared in case friends and family paid us a visit, which they invariably did.

This gracious hospitality is typical of the Middle East. The custom can be traced back through centuries, as can the dishes themselves. The Arab word for hors d'oeuvre, for example, is *mezze*, which comes from the Greek *maza* (porridge), a word which embraces taramasalata, houmus and many similar dishes found in both Greek and Middle Eastern cuisines.

While many Middle Eastern dishes have similar origins, every region, every country, every town, and, in days gone by, every family, had their own recipes, their own way of preparing a universal dish. What was known by one name in one country was called something completely different in another. Certain regions have, however, become associated with specific dishes. The Persian *khoresh* is especially interesting, as it can be traced back over two centuries to the time of the Parthians. Their concept of good and evil was reflected in their food.

Dishes like *khoreshe hoo*, a blend of lamb with peas and prunes, and *khoreshe ghoureh*, meat with nuts, vinegar and sour grapes, express the Parthian belief in the eternal battle between light and darkness. This balance continues to be the basis of Persian cuisine, although it is doubtful if many cooks are aware of its origins as they prepare *khoresh* in kitchens throughout the world.

Rice is one of the staples of Middle Eastern cuisine, but this was not always the case. The diet originally consisted of millet porridge, coarse bread, olives, figs, beans, cheese and milk. Rice was a luxury, grown on the northern borders of Persia around the Caspian Sea. Gradually it became available to the more wealthy urban dwellers, but it took centuries for rice to become universally adopted. Nowadays we are spoilt for choice with basmati rice and the American long grain varieties, but nothing beats rice from Iran. Its smell, texture and flavour are unique and have to be experienced to be believed. No other Middle Eastern Country prepares rice as the Iranians do; cooking rice to perfection is almost a matter of national pride.

Other important ingredients include milk, honey, yogurt, cheese, fruit and vegetables, especially garlic and onions. Olive oil has long been recognised in the Middle East for its healthy properties. Meat and poultry are valued for their protein content, and if meat is not used, dried beans and other pulses are substituted.

*Freshly picked, ripe cherries are offered for sale from this roadside stall in a bustling Damascus street market near the shores of the Mediterranean.*

What you will not find in these pages are any recipes which feature pork. The reasons would seem obvious, but the roots are not religious. Had this book been written four centuries ago, pork would have been central to the cuisine, as the pig was a favoured animal throughout the region. It was only the invasion of the Indo-Aryan tribes around 2000 BC that signalled its departure. The Indo-Aryans were cattle-rearers. They disliked pigs, which were hard to herd, and which they found offensive due to the dirty conditions the pigs revelled in. It was also very difficult to keep the meat fresh in the heat. The days of the pigs were numbered and they have in fact never returned.

Puddings and desserts are not common in the Middle East. The main courses tend to be very filling, so fruit is generally preferred at the end of a meal. Sweetmeats are served on festive occasions, or when entertaining guests for tea.

In the past cooking fats used in the preparation of Middle Eastern dishes tended to be quite heavy. The *alya* or fat from a sheep's or lamb's tail, was particularly popular. Since finding a sheep's or lamb's tail in the local supermarket can be a problem nowadays, I have substituted cooking oil, and in some cases, butter. I've taken similar liberties with other ingredients which I am sure my grandmother would never have countenanced in her dishes, but it's a question of needs must, especially when the ingredients have to be sourced from Western shops. Through-out the book, however, I've been careful to retain each dish's unique flavour despite minor changes to accommodate the Western palate.

The other aspect I am most aware of is that the dishes must be easy to prepare. Commonsense and creativity have been my watchwords. Naturally there is an element of hard work in making some of the dishes, but I have

*In an Israeli market stall, piled high with dried dates and sweets, a child minds the store.*

streamlined the processes where possible. I am not afraid of using modern labour-saving devices such as the blender, or using bought ingredients. My grandmother, for example, would have made her own yogurt. I confess that I do not.

As the mother of two teenage daughters and with a husband who is forever hungry, cooking is a necessity, but one which, over the years, has become ever more enjoyable. When I embarked on my culinary journey many years ago on marrying an English husband, meals were a hit-and-miss affair, but he encouraged me to continue, always praising my cooking and telling me how delicious each dish

was. The occasional international telephone call to Tehran to ask my mother how to make a certain dish, or the odd times when everything went wrong are now dim memories, but I would happily go through the learning process again.

With the aid of this book I hope everyone will be able to cook their favourite meals for themselves and experiment with other dishes.

Writing this book and sharing my joy of food with you all has been immensely satisfying and my only regret is that I cannot personally share each and every one of your dishes and see the smiles when they are presented at the dinner table.

# INGREDIENTS

A walk through the bazaar in Tehran provides a wonderful introduction to Middle Eastern ingredients. Shop after shop is packed with aromatics and spices, from rose petals to cinnamon and saffron. You can buy any combination you choose, but the most popular herbs and spices are chives, cinnamon, paprika, saffron and turmeric.

## AUBERGINE
There are countless ways of preparing this incomparable vegetable, but the secret of preserving the delicate flavour lies in removing any bitterness. This is done by slicing or dicing the aubergine into a colander, sprinkling it with salt and allowing it to drain. It is rinsed and dried before use.

## BROAD BEANS
Broad beans are available frozen from any supermarket or fresh when in season. Only the tender green centre of the bean is used in Middle Eastern cooking, so they need to be shelled if frozen or podded and shelled if fresh. When the fresh beans are cooked with rice and dill for *baghali polo*, they add an exquisite taste and aroma to the dish.

## CINNAMON
The powdered form of this spice is widely used in all sorts of Middle Eastern recipes, especially in different types of *khoresh*.

Clockwise from top left: garlic, two varieties of aubergines, broad beans (in the shell and loose), baby spinach, vine leaves and red pepper (centre).

Dried limes and *zereshk* (on board) with (from left), short grain rice, basmati and long grain rice.

## CUMIN
The delicate aroma of the spice is a perfect complement to many vegetable dishes and salads. It is also used in Gulf fish curries. Cumin seeds have a flavour similar to that of caraway. In Middle Eastern cooking cumin is used either whole or ground.

## DRIED LIMES
*Limu amani* are available from Middle Eastern or Greek shops, either whole or crushed, and make a very good alternative to lemon. They are usually cooked with meat and fresh herbs.

## GARLIC
Used extensively throughout the Middle East, garlic is valued for its health properties as well as its flavour.

## HERBS
Chives, coriander, dill, marjoram, mint and parsley are among the most important ingredients in any Middle Eastern kitchen. They are served fresh, traditionally on a separate plate to accompany the food. Fresh herbs are offered with cheese, cooked with meat and rice, mixed into salads and used in stuffings for vegetables. Chopped herbs are used in handfuls, rather than spoonfuls, in all sorts of cooked dishes.

## NUTMEG
Whole nutmegs are the hard aromatic seeds of an evergreen tree. The spice is widely used all over the world. Whole nutmegs can be grated for cooking, but in Middle Eastern dishes it is most usual to use the ground spice.

A selection of nuts, clockwise from top left: (on board) pine nuts, hazelnuts and almonds; walnuts and pistachio nuts.

## NUTS
Nuts are widely used in Middle Eastern cooking and are often combined with rice, but how they are used depends on the country. In Iran, for instance, walnuts are ground, cooked with either chicken or duck and made into a delicious sauce with pomegranate juice or sour cherries. Almonds, hazelnuts, pistachios and pine nuts are not only combined with rice and used in savoury stuffings, but are also used to fill sweetmeats such as baklava.

## PAPRIKA
Although paprika is often associated with Eastern Europe it is widely used in the Middle East in soups, meat dishes, salad dressings and garnishes.

## RED PEPPERS
Widely used, red peppers make a delicious meal when stuffed or cooked with meat and aubergines. When grilled, they acquire a smoky flavour, and are a tasty salad ingredient.

## RICE
Rice is the most common ingredient in Middle Eastern cooking. Basmati rice has an exquisite taste and aroma. Long grain American rice gives adequate results, while short grain rice is mainly used for puddings.

## SAFFRON
Derived from the dried stamens of a type of crocus, saffron has a superb aroma and flavour. It also adds a delicate colour to food. For the best results it should be ground to a powder and diluted in a small amount of boiling water.

## SPINACH
Fresh baby spinach leaves are available from greengrocers and supermarkets throughout the year. In the Midde East, spinach is often cooked with meat or combined with yogurt to make a popular vegetarian starter.

## SUMAC
These edible red berries are dried and crushed to a powder and are delicious sprinkled on kebabs, fish dishes and all sorts of salads.

## TURMERIC
This spice originated in Iran. It adds a distinctive flavour and rich yellow colour to meat and rice dishes. It is widely used throughout the Middle East and India.

A selection of spices, left to right from top row: ground *sumac*, saffron threads, paprika, cinnamon sticks, turmeric, cardamom pods, ground nutmeg, whole nutmegs and cumin seeds.

## VINE LEAVES
When stuffed with meat, lentils and herbs, these make delicious starters.

## ZERESHK
This is a small sour berry that grows on trees by the water in the warmer part of Iran. It is traditionally served with Persian rice dishes.

A selection of fresh herbs, clockwise from top left: dill, flat leaf parsley, mint, marjoram and coriander (centre).

# SOUPS
# AND
# STARTERS

*It is for mezze – the marvellous array of hot and cold dishes served as starters – that the Middle East is particularly well known. A special meal may commence with a selection of twenty or more, from a simple spinach and yogurt salad to wedges of a complex herb and vegetable egg pie. Taramasalata, Houmus, and Aubergine and Tahini Dip are delicious when scooped up with pitta bread, while tiny pastries, stuffed vegetables and salads complete the spread. In addition to chilled yogurt-based soups, the chapter includes some winter warmers.*

# Beef and Herb Soup with Yogurt

This classic Iranian soup, *Aashe Maste*, is almost a meal in itself. It is full of invigorating herbs, and is a popular cold weather dish.

## INGREDIENTS

*Serves 6*
2 large onions
30ml/2 tbsp oil
15ml/1 tbsp ground turmeric
100g/3½ oz/½ cup yellow split peas
1.2 litres/2 pints/5 cups water
225g/8oz minced beef
200g/7oz/1 cup rice
45ml/3 tbsp each fresh chopped
    parsley, coriander and chives
15g/½ oz/1 tbsp butter
1 large garlic clove, finely chopped
60ml/4 tbsp chopped mint
2–3 saffron strands dissolved in
    15ml/1 tbsp boiling water (optional)
salt and freshly ground black pepper
yogurt and naan bread, to serve

*1* Chop one of the onions then heat the oil in a large saucepan and fry the onion until golden brown. Add the turmeric, split peas and water, bring to the boil, then reduce the heat and simmer for 20 minutes.

— COOK'S TIP —

Fresh spinach is also delicious in this soup. Add 50g/2oz finely chopped spinach leaves to the soup with the parsley, coriander and chives.

*2* Grate the other onion into a bowl, add the minced beef and seasoning and mix well. Using your hands, form the mixture into small balls, about the size of walnuts. Carefully add to the pan and simmer for 10 minutes.

*3* Add the rice, then stir in the parsley, coriander, and chives and simmer for about 30 minutes, until the rice is tender, stirring frequently.

*4* Melt the butter in a small pan and gently fry the garlic. Add the mint, stir briefly and sprinkle over the soup with the saffron, if using.

*5* Spoon the soup into warmed serving dishes and serve with yogurt and naan bread.

# Spinach and Lemon Soup with Meatballs

*Aarshe Saak* is almost standard fare in many parts of the Middle East. In Greece it is normally made without the meatballs and is called Avgolemono.

## INGREDIENTS

*Serves 6*
2 large onions
45ml/3 tbsp oil
15ml/1 tbsp ground turmeric
100g/3½ oz/½ cup yellow split peas
1.2 litres/2 pints/5 cups water
225g/8oz minced lamb
450g/1lb spinach, chopped
50g/2oz/½ cup rice flour
juice of 2 lemons
1–2 garlic cloves, very
   finely chopped
30ml/2 tbsp chopped fresh mint
4 eggs, beaten
salt and freshly ground black pepper

*1* Chop one of the onions, heat 30ml/2 tbsp of the oil in a large frying pan and fry the onion until golden. Add the turmeric, split peas and water and bring to the boil. Reduce the heat and simmer for 20 minutes.

*2* Grate the other onion. Put it into a bowl, add the minced lamb and seasoning and mix well. Using your hands, form the mixture into small balls, about the size of walnuts. Carefully add to the pan and simmer for 10 minutes, then add the chopped spinach, cover and simmer for 20 minutes.

*3* Mix the flour with about 250ml/ 8fl oz/1 cup cold water to make a smooth paste, then slowly add to the pan, stirring all the time to prevent lumps. Stir in the lemon juice, season with salt and pepper and cook over a gentle heat for 20 minutes.

*4* Meanwhile, heat the remaining oil in a small pan and fry the garlic briefly until golden. Stir in the mint and remove the pan from the heat.

*5* Remove the soup from the heat and stir in the beaten eggs. Sprinkle the garlic and mint garnish over the soup and serve.

---

COOK'S TIP

If preferred, use less lemon juice to begin with and then add more to taste once the soup is cooked.

# Spinach and Yogurt Borani

This popular starter from Iran, called *Borani Esfanaj*, is as simple as it is healthy.

## INGREDIENTS

*Serves 4*
25g/1oz/2 tbsp butter or margarine
1 large onion, chopped
2 garlic cloves, crushed
450g/1lb fresh spinach, chopped
475ml/16fl oz/2 cups natural yogurt
salt and freshly ground black pepper

—————— COOK'S TIP ——————

Use 225g/8oz thawed, frozen spinach if fresh spinach is not available.

*1* Melt the butter or margarine in a large saucepan and fry the onion until golden brown. Add the garlic and chopped spinach and continue frying, stirring occasionally. The spinach will cook in its own moisture. Continue cooking over a low heat until all the moisture has evaporated.

*2* Stir the yogurt into the spinach mixture. Season with salt and pepper, mix well and then allow to cool completely before serving.

# Lentil Soup

This traditional Turkish soup makes an ideal winter starter.

## INGREDIENTS

*Serves 4*
45ml/3 tbsp olive oil
1 large onion, chopped
1 celery stick, chopped
400g/14oz/2½ cups red lentils
1.2 litres/2 pints/5 cups meat stock
4–5 tomatoes
juice of 1 lemon
2.5ml/½ tsp chilli powder (optional)
salt and freshly ground black pepper

*1* Heat the oil in a large saucepan and cook the onion and celery over a gentle heat until soft. Add the lentils and stock to the pan, bring to the boil and then simmer for 25 minutes until the lentils are soft.

*2* Peel the tomatoes, by dipping them into boiling water for about 30 seconds to loosen the skins.

*3* Chop the tomatoes roughly on a chopping board with a sharp knife, and add to the pan with the lemon juice, salt and pepper and the chilli powder, if using. Simmer for a further 10 minutes and serve.

—————— COOK'S TIP ——————

Yellow and/or brown lentils can be used instead of red lentils, if preferred. They may require slightly longer to cook.

# Dolmeh

*Dolmeh*, meaning "stuffed" in Persian, generally refers to any vegetable or fruit stuffed with meat, rice and herbs. It is a favourite dish throughout the Middle East.

## INGREDIENTS

*Serves 4–6*
250g/9oz vine leaves
30ml/2 tbsp olive oil
1 large onion, finely chopped
250g/9oz minced lamb
50g/2oz/¼ cup yellow split peas
75g/3oz/½ cup cooked rice
30ml/2 tbsp chopped fresh parsley
30ml/2 tbsp chopped fresh mint
30ml/2 tbsp snipped fresh chives
3–4 spring onions, finely chopped
juice of 2 lemons
30ml/2 tbsp tomato purée (optional)
30ml/2 tbsp sugar
salt and freshly ground black pepper
yogurt and pitta bread, to serve

*1* Blanch fresh vine leaves if using, in boiling water for 1–2 minutes to soften them, or rinse preserved bottled or canned vine leaves under cold water.

*2* Heat the olive oil in a large frying pan and fry the onion for a few minutes until slightly softened. Add the meat and fry over a moderate heat until well browned, stirring frequently. Season with salt and pepper.

*3* Place the split peas in a small pan with enough water to cover and bring to the boil. Cover the pan and simmer gently over a low heat for 12–15 minutes until soft. Drain the split peas if necessary.

*4* Stir the split peas, cooked rice, chopped herbs, spring onions, and the juice of one of the lemons into the meat. Add the tomato purée, if using, and then knead the mixture with your hands until thoroughly blended.

*5* Place a vine leaf on a chopping board with the vein side up. Place 15ml/1 tbsp of the meat mixture on the vine leaf and fold the stem end over the meat. Fold the sides in towards the centre and then fold over to make a neat parcel. Continue until all the filling has been used up.

*6* Line the base of a large saucepan with several unstuffed leaves and arrange the rolled leaves in tight layers on top. Stir the remaining lemon juice and the sugar into about 150ml/¼ pint/ ⅔ cup water and pour over the leaves. Place a small heat resistant plate over the *dolmeh* to keep them in shape. Cover the pan with a tight-fitting lid and cook over a very low heat for 2 hours, checking occasionally and adding a little extra water should the pan begin to boil dry. Serve warm or cold with yogurt and warm pitta bread.

---

COOK'S TIP

If using preserved vine leaves, soak them overnight in cold water and then rinse several times before use.

---

# Stuffed Peppers

Stuffed peppers or *Dolmeh Felfel* make a tasty and attractive starter, especially when all four colours of pepper are used.

### INGREDIENTS

*Serves 6*

6 mixed peppers (red, yellow and green)
30ml/2 tbsp olive oil
1 large onion, finely chopped
3–4 spring onions, finely chopped
250g/9oz minced lamb
2 garlic cloves, crushed (optional)
50g/2oz/¼ cup yellow split peas
75g/3oz/½ cup cooked rice
30ml/2 tbsp finely chopped fresh parsley
30ml/2 tbsp finely chopped fresh mint
30ml/2 tbsp finely snipped fresh chives
5ml/1 tsp ground cinnamon
juice of 2 lemons
30ml/2 tbsp tomato purée (optional)
400g/14oz can chopped tomatoes
knob of butter
salt and freshly ground black pepper
yogurt and pitta bread or naan, to serve

*1* Cut off the mixed pepper tops and set aside. Remove the seeds and cores and trim the bases so they stand squarely. Cook in boiling salted water for 5 minutes, then drain, rinse under cold water and set aside.

*2* Heat the oil in a large saucepan or flameproof casserole and fry the onion and spring onions for about 4–5 minutes until golden brown. Add the meat and fry over a moderate heat until well browned, stirring frequently. Stir in the garlic if using.

*3* Place the split peas in a small pan with enough water to cover, bring to the boil and then simmer gently for 12–15 minutes until soft. Drain.

*4* Stir the split peas, cooked rice, herbs, cinnamon, juice of one of the lemons, and the tomato purée, if using, into the meat. Season with salt and pepper and stir again until all are well combined.

*5* Spoon the rice and split pea mixture into the peppers and place the reserved lids on top.

*6* Pour the chopped tomatoes into a large saucepan or flameproof casserole and add the remaining lemon juice and butter. Arrange the peppers neatly in the pan with the stems upwards. Bring to the boil and then cover tightly and cook over a low heat for 40–45 minutes until the peppers are tender.

*7* Serve the peppers with the tomato sauce accompanied by yogurt and warm pitta bread or naan.

---

COOK'S TIP

Make sure that the saucepan or casserole that you choose is just large enough so that the peppers fit quite snugly.

# Fattoush

This simple peasant salad has become a popular dish all over Syria and the Lebanon.

## INGREDIENTS

*Serves 4*

1 yellow or red pepper
1 large cucumber
4–5 tomatoes
1 bunch spring onions
30ml/2 tbsp finely chopped
   fresh parsley
30ml/2 tbsp finely chopped fresh mint
30ml/2 tbsp finely chopped
   fresh coriander
2 garlic cloves, crushed
75ml/5 tbsp olive oil
juice of 2 lemons
salt and freshly ground black pepper
2 pitta breads

*1* Slice the pepper, discarding the seeds and core, then roughly chop the cucumber and tomatoes. Place them in a large salad bowl.

*2* Trim and slice the spring onions. Add to the cucumber, tomatoes and pepper with the finely chopped parsley, mint and coriander.

*3* To make the dressing, blend the garlic with the olive oil and lemon juice in a jug, then season to taste with salt and black pepper. Pour the dressing over the salad and toss lightly to mix.

*4* Toast the pitta bread in a toaster or under a hot grill until crisp and then serve it alongside the salad.

---
VARIATION
---

If you prefer, make this salad in the traditional way. After toasting the pitta bread until crisp, crush it in your hand and then sprinkle it over the salad before serving.

---
COOK'S TIP
---

Although the recipe calls for only 30ml/ 2 tbsp of each of the herbs, if you have plenty to hand, then you can add as much as you like to this aromatic salad.

# Baked Eggs with Herbs and Vegetables

Eggs, baked or fried as omelettes with vegetables and herbs and sometimes meat, too, are popular throughout the Middle East. This particular dish, *Kuku Sabzi*, comes from Persia and is a traditional New Year favourite.

## INGREDIENTS

*Serves 4–6*
2–3 saffron strands
8 eggs
2 leeks
115g/4oz fresh spinach
½ iceberg lettuce
4 spring onions
45ml/3 tbsp chopped fresh parsley
45ml/3 tbsp snipped fresh chives
45ml/3 tbsp chopped fresh coriander
1 garlic clove, crushed
30ml/2 tbsp chopped walnuts
   (optional)
25g/1oz/2 tbsp butter
salt and freshly ground black pepper
yogurt and pitta bread, to serve

*1* Preheat the oven to 180°C/350°F/ Gas 4. Soak the saffron strands in 15ml/1 tbsp boiling water.

---
COOK'S TIP
---

To bring out their flavour, lightly toast the walnuts in a moderate oven, or under a hot grill before chopping.

*2* Beat the eggs in a large bowl. Chop the leeks, spinach, lettuce and spring onions finely and add to the eggs together with the chopped herbs, garlic, and walnuts, if using. Season with salt and pepper, add the saffron water and stir thoroughly to mix.

*3* Melt the butter in a large ovenproof dish and pour in the vegetable and egg mixture.

*4* Bake in the oven for 35–40 minutes until the egg mixture is set and the top is golden. Serve hot or cold, cut into wedges, with yogurt and pitta bread.

# Böreks

In Turkey, little stuffed pasties are very popular. They are easy to make and are ideal for starters, parties or finger canapés.

## INGREDIENTS

*Makes 35–40*
225g/8oz feta cheese, grated
225g/8oz mozzarella, grated
2 eggs, beaten
45ml/3 tbsp chopped fresh parsley
45ml/3 tbsp snipped fresh chives
45ml/3 tbsp chopped fresh mint
pinch of nutmeg
225g/8oz filo pastry
45–60ml/3–4 tbsp melted butter
freshly ground black pepper

*1* Preheat the oven to 180°C/350°F/ Gas 4. In a bowl, blend the feta and mozzarella cheeses with the beaten eggs. Add the chopped herbs, season with black pepper and nutmeg, and stir well to mix.

*2* Cut the sheets of pastry into four rectangular strips approximately 7.5cm/3in wide. Cover all but one or two strips of the pastry with a damp cloth to prevent them from drying out.

*3* Brush one strip of pastry at a time with a little melted butter.

*4* Place 5ml/1 tsp of filling at the bottom edge. Fold one corner over the filling to make a triangle shape. Continue folding the pastry over itself until you get to the end of the strip. Keep making triangles until all the mixture is used up.

*5* Place the *böreks* on a greased baking tray and bake in the oven for about 30 minutes until golden brown and crisp. Serve warm or cold.

---
COOK'S TIP
---

A mixture of almost any cheeses can be used but avoid cream cheeses.

# Aubergine and Tahini Dip

This Turkish variation of a popular Middle Eastern dish is said to have been invented by the ladies of the sultan's harem – to win his favour.

## INGREDIENTS

*Serves 4–6*
3 aubergines
2 garlic cloves, crushed
60ml/4 tbsp tahini paste
juice of 2 lemons
15ml/1 tbsp paprika
salt and freshly ground black pepper
chopped fresh parsley, olive oil plus a
    few olives, to garnish
pitta bread or crudités, to serve

*1* Preheat the oven to 190°C/375°F/ Gas 5. Slit the skins of the aubergines, place on a baking sheet and bake in the oven for 30–40 minutes until the skins begin to split.

*2* Place the aubergines on a chopping board. Carefully peel away the skins from the aubergines.

*3* Place the aubergine flesh in a blender or food processor. Add the garlic, tahini paste, lemon juice, paprika and salt and pepper. Blend to a smooth paste, adding about 15–30ml/1–2 tbsp water if the paste is too thick.

*4* Spoon into a dish and make a dip in the centre. Garnish with paprika, chopped parsley, a drizzle of olive oil and olives. Serve with hot pitta bread or a selection of crudités.

---
COOK'S TIP

Tahini paste can be obtained from health food shops and delicatessens.

---

# Aubergines with Tomatoes and Eggs

*Mirza Ghasemi* is a speciality of northern Iran. Serve it with warm pitta bread for an unusual lunch or as a starter.

## INGREDIENTS

*Serves 4–6*

4 aubergines
115g/4oz/½ cup butter or margarine
1 large onion, finely chopped
2 garlic cloves, crushed
4 large tomatoes, peeled, seeded and chopped
4 eggs
salt and freshly ground black pepper

---
COOK'S TIP
---

Peel the tomatoes by dipping them in boiling water to loosen the skins.

*1* Preheat the oven to 190°C/375°F/ Gas 5. Carefully slit the skins of the aubergines, place them on a baking sheet and bake in the oven for 30–40 minutes until the skins begin to split.

*2* Meanwhile, melt 50g/2oz/4 tbsp of the butter or margarine in a large frying pan and fry the onion and garlic for 4–5 minutes until softened. Add the tomatoes and fry for a further 2–3 minutes.

*3* Peel the aubergines, finely chop the flesh and stir into the pan with the onion and tomatoes. Cook for about 4–5 minutes, stirring frequently.

*4* Melt the remaining butter or margarine in a small frying pan, add the beaten eggs and cook over a low heat until the eggs are just beginning to set, stirring occasionally with a fork. Stir the eggs into the aubergine mixture, season to taste and serve.

# Taramasalata

This delicious Turkish and Greek speciality makes an excellent starter.

## INGREDIENTS

*Serves 4*

115g/4oz smoked mullet roe
2 garlic cloves, crushed
30ml/2 tbsp grated onion
60ml/4 tbsp olive oil
4 slices white bread, crusts removed
juice of 2 lemons
30ml/2 tbsp water or milk
paprika, to garnish (optional)

---
COOK'S TIP
---

Since the roe of grey mullet is expensive, smoked cod's roe is often used instead for this dish. It is paler than the burnt-orange colour of mullet roe but is still very good.

*1* Place the smoked mullet roe, garlic, onion, olive oil, bread and lemon juice in a blender or food processor and process until smooth.

*2* Add the water or milk and process again for a few seconds. (This will give the taramasalata a creamier taste.)

*3* Pour the taramasalata into a serving bowl, cover with clear film and chill for 1–2 hours before serving. Just before serving, sprinkle with a little paprika, if liked.

# Falafel

These tasty deep fried patties are one of the national dishes of Egypt. They make an excellent starter or else can be served as a buffet dish.

### INGREDIENTS

*Serves 6*
450g/1lb/2½ cups dried white beans
2 red onions, chopped
2 large garlic cloves, crushed
45ml/3 tbsp finely chopped fresh
  parsley
5ml/1 tsp ground coriander
5ml/1 tsp ground cumin
7.5ml/1½ tsp baking powder
oil, for deep frying
salt and freshly ground black pepper
tomato salad, to serve

*1* Soak the white beans overnight in water. Remove the skins and process in a blender or food processor. Add the chopped onions, garlic, parsley, coriander, cumin, baking powder and seasoning and blend again to make a very smooth paste. Allow the mixture to stand at room temperature for at least 30 minutes.

*2* Take walnut-sized pieces of mixture and flatten into small patties. Set aside again for about 15 minutes.

*3* Heat the oil until it's very hot and then fry the patties in batches until golden brown. Drain on kitchen paper and then serve with a tomato salad.

# Houmus

This popular Middle Eastern dip is widely available in supermarkets, but nothing compares with the delicious home-made variety.

### INGREDIENTS

*Serves 4–6*
175g/6oz/1 cup cooked chick-peas
120ml/4fl oz/½ cup tahini paste
3 garlic cloves
juice of 2 lemons
45–60ml/3–4 tbsp water
salt and freshly ground black pepper
fresh radishes, to serve

**For the garnish**
15ml/1 tbsp olive oil
15ml/1 tbsp finely chopped fresh
  parsley
2.5ml/½ tsp paprika
4 black olives

*1* Place the chick-peas, tahini paste, garlic, lemon juice, seasoning and a little of the water in a blender or food processor. Process until smooth adding a little more water, if necessary.

*2* Alternatively if you don't have a blender or food processor, mix the ingredients together in a small bowl until smooth in consistency.

*3* Spoon the mixture into a shallow dish. Make a dent in the middle and pour the olive oil into it. Garnish with parsley, paprika and olives and serve with the radishes.

----

COOK'S TIP

Canned chick-peas can be used for houmus. Drain and rinse under cold water before processing.

# MEAT DISHES

*Lamb and beef feature strongly on Middle Eastern menus. This chapter includes well-known dishes like kebabs, couscous and koftas, but also introduces the delicious range of stews known in Iran as* khoresh, *which combine various types of meat or poultry with fruits, herbs and spices. Long, slow cooking allows the flavours to blend to produce a delicious mellow result. Stewing and grilling are the most popular cooking methods, but where meat is roasted or sautéed, it is often marinated in yogurt for tenderness and extra flavour.*

# Tangy Beef and Herb Khoresh

Lamb, beef or poultry stews combined with vegetables, fruit, herbs and spices, are called *khoresh* in Farsi and are among the most loved of Persian dishes. Like this beef stew, *Khoreshe Gormeh Sabzi*, they are mildly spiced and are ideal for a simple but delicious dinner party.

## INGREDIENTS

*Serves 4*

45ml/3 tbsp oil
1 large onion, chopped
450g/1lb lean stewing beef, cubed
15ml/1 tbsp fenugreek leaf
10ml/2 tsp ground turmeric
2.5ml/½ tsp ground cinnamon
600ml/1 pint/2½ cups water
25g/1oz fresh parsley, chopped
25g/1oz fresh chives, snipped
425g/15oz can red kidney beans
juice of 1 lemon
salt and freshly ground black pepper
rice, to serve

1 Heat 30ml/2 tbsp of the oil in a large saucepan or flameproof casserole and fry the onion for about 3–4 minutes until lightly golden. Add the beef and fry for a further 5–10 minutes until browned, stirring so that the meat browns on all sides.

2 Add the fenugreek, turmeric and cinnamon and cook for about 1 minute, stirring, then add the water and bring to the boil. Cover and simmer over a low heat for 45 minutes, stirring occasionally.

3 Heat the remaining oil in a small frying pan and fry the parsley and chives over a moderate heat for 2–3 minutes, stirring frequently.

4 Drain the kidney beans and stir them into the beef with the herbs and lemon juice. Season with salt and pepper. Simmer the stew for a further 30–35 minutes, until the meat is tender. Serve on a bed of rice.

# Lamb with Split Peas

*Khoreshe Ghaimeh* is another traditional Persian dish and is always served at parties and religious ceremonies. It is a great favourite with children too!

### INGREDIENTS

*Serves 4*

25g/1oz/2 tbsp butter or margarine
1 large onion, chopped
450g/1lb lean lamb, cut into
    small cubes
5ml/1 tsp ground turmeric
5ml/1 tsp ground cinnamon
5ml/1 tsp curry powder
300ml/½ pint/1¼ cups water
2–3 saffron strands
100g/3½oz/½ cup yellow split peas
3 *limu amani* (dried limes)
3–4 tomatoes, chopped
30ml/2 tbsp oil
2 large potatoes, chopped
salt and freshly ground black pepper
rice, to serve

*1* Melt the butter or margarine in a large saucepan or flameproof casserole and fry the onion for 3–4 minutes until golden, stirring occasionally. Add the meat and cook over a high heat for a further 3–4 minutes until it has browned.

*2* Add the turmeric, cinnamon and curry powder and cook for about 2 minutes, stirring frequently.

*3* Stir in the water, season well and bring to the boil, then cover and simmer over a low heat for about 30–35 minutes, until the meat is half cooked. Stir the saffron into about 15ml/1 tbsp boiling water.

*4* Add the saffron to the meat with the split peas, *limu amani* and tomatoes. Stir well and then simmer, covered, for a further 35 minutes until the meat is completely tender.

*5* Heat the oil in a frying pan and fry the potatoes for 10–15 minutes, until cooked and golden. Lift out the *limu amani* and discard. Spoon the meat on to a large serving dish and scatter the potatoes on top. Serve the *khoresh* with rice.

---
COOK'S TIP
---

*Limu amani* (dried limes) are available in all Persian or Middle Eastern shops. However, if you have difficulty obtaining them, use the juice of either 2 limes or 1 lemon instead. If you prefer, you can use lean stewing beef in place of the lamb in this traditional *khoresh*.

# Lamb and Celery Khoresh

This unusual stew, *Khoreshe Karafs*, has a lovely fresh taste.

**INGREDIENTS**

*Serves 4*
1 large onion, chopped
40g/1½ oz/3 tbsp butter
450g/1lb lean lamb, cubed
5ml/1 tsp ground turmeric
2.5ml/½ tsp ground cinnamon
600ml/1 pint/2½ cups water
1 head of celery, chopped
25g/1oz fresh parsley, chopped
1 small bunch of fresh mint, chopped
juice of 1 lemon
salt and freshly ground black pepper
mint leaves, to garnish
rice, and cucumber and tomato
    salad, to serve

*1* Fry the onion in 25g/1oz/2 tbsp of the butter in a large saucepan or flameproof casserole for 3–4 minutes.

*2* Add the meat and cook for 2–3 minutes until browned, stirring frequently, then stir in the turmeric, cinnamon and salt and pepper.

*3* Add the water and bring to the boil, then reduce the heat, cover and simmer for about 30 minutes until the meat is half cooked.

*4* Melt the remaining butter in a frying pan and fry the celery for 8–10 minutes, until tender, stirring frequently. Add the parsley and mint and fry for a further 3–4 minutes.

*5* Stir the celery and herbs together with the lemon juice into the meat and simmer, covered, for a further 25–30 minutes until the meat is completely tender. Serve garnished with mint leaves and accompanied by rice and a cucumber and tomato salad.

---
COOK'S TIP

If you prefer, this dish can be made with canned or chopped fresh tomatoes in place of some of the herbs. Add the tomatoes in step 4 at the same time as the celery.

---

# Lamb with Spinach and Prunes

If you like fresh spinach you will love this delicious, lightly spiced, sweet and sour dish known as *Khoreshe Esanaj*.

**INGREDIENTS**

*Serves 4*
45ml/3 tbsp oil
1 large onion, chopped
450g/1lb lean lamb, cubed
2.5ml/½ tsp grated nutmeg
5ml/1 tsp ground cinnamon
600ml/1 pint/2½ cups water
150g/5oz chives or spring onions,
    including green parts, finely chopped
450g/1lb fresh spinach, chopped
250g/9oz/1¾ cups prunes, soaked
juice of 1 lemon
salt and freshly ground black pepper
rice, to serve

*1* Heat 30ml/2 tbsp of the oil and fry the onion for 3–4 minutes until golden. Add the lamb and fry until brown on all sides, then sprinkle over the nutmeg and cinnamon and stir well.

*2* Add the water, bring to the boil and spoon off any scum that rises to the surface. Season with salt and pepper and then cover and simmer over a low heat for 40–45 minutes until the meat is nearly cooked.

*3* Heat the remaining oil in another large pan, add the chives or spring onions, stir fry for a few minutes and then add the spinach. Cover and cook over a moderate heat for 2–3 minutes until the spinach has wilted and then add this mixture to the meat, with the prunes and lemon juice.

*4* Cook, covered, for a further 20–25 minutes, until the meat is completely tender. Serve with rice.

# Minced Meat Kebabs

In the Middle East, these kebabs are known as *Kabab Kobideh* and are often served with rice into which is stirred raw egg yolk and melted butter. Traditionally, they are barbecued, but can also be cooked under a hot grill.

## INGREDIENTS

*Serves 6–8*

450g/1lb lean lamb
450g/1lb lean beef
1 large onion, grated
2 garlic cloves, crushed
15ml/1 tbsp *sumac* (optional)
10ml/2 tsp bicarbonate of soda
2–3 saffron strands, soaked in
    15ml/1 tbsp boiling water
6–8 tomatoes, halved
15ml/1 tbsp melted butter
salt and freshly ground black pepper

1 Mince the lamb and beef two or three times until very finely minced, place in a large bowl and add the grated onion, garlic, *sumac*, if using, soaked saffron, bicarbonate of soda and salt and pepper.

2 Knead by hand for several minutes until the mixture is very glutinous. It helps to have a bowl of water nearby in which to dip your fingers to stop the meat sticking.

3 Take a small handful of meat and roll it into a ball. If the ball seems crumbly, knead the mixture in the bowl for a few more minutes.

4 Shape the ball around a flat skewer, moulding it around the skewer. Repeat with three or four more balls on each skewer, pressing them tightly to prevent the meat from falling off.

5 Thread the tomatoes on to separate skewers and prepare a barbecue.

6 When the coals are ready, grill the meat and tomato kebabs for about 10 minutes, basting them with the melted butter and turning occasionally.

---
COOK'S TIP
---

*Sumac* is a favourite Lebanese spice with a slightly sour but fruity flavour. It is available from most Middle Eastern food shops, but it is not essential in this recipe.

# Sautéed Lamb with Yogurt

In the Middle East meat is normally stewed or barbecued. Here's a delicious exception from Turkey where the lamb is pan-fried instead.

## INGREDIENTS

*Serves 4*

450g/1lb lean lamb, preferably boned leg, cubed
40g/1½oz/3 tbsp butter
4 tomatoes, skinned and chopped
4 thick slices of bread, crusts removed
250ml/8fl oz/1 cup Greek yogurt
2 garlic cloves, crushed
salt and freshly ground black pepper
paprika and mint leaves, to garnish

**For the marinade**
120ml/4fl oz/½ cup Greek yogurt
1 large onion, grated

*1* First make the marinade: blend together the yogurt, onion and a little seasoning in a large bowl. Add the cubed lamb, cover loosely with clear film and leave to marinate in a cool place for at least 1 hour.

*2* Melt half the butter in a frying pan and fry the meat for 5–10 minutes, until tender but still moist. Transfer to a plate with a slotted spoon and keep warm while cooking the tomatoes.

*3* Melt the remaining butter in the same pan and fry the tomatoes for 4–5 minutes until soft. Meanwhile, toast the bread and arrange in the bottom of a shallow serving dish.

*4* Season the tomatoes and then spread over the toasted bread in an even layer.

*5* Blend the yogurt and garlic and season with salt and pepper. Spoon over the tomatoes.

*6* Arrange the meat in a layer on top. Sprinkle with paprika and mint leaves and serve at once.

# Persian Kebabs

Kebabs are eaten throughout the Middle East and almost always cooked over a wood or charcoal fire. There are many variations; this particular recipe, *Kabab Bahrg*, comes from Iran and many restaurants serve only this dish.

## INGREDIENTS

*Serves 4*
450g/1lb lean lamb or beef fillet
2–3 saffron strands
1 large onion, grated
4–6 tomatoes, halved
15ml/1 tbsp butter, melted
salt and freshly ground black pepper
45ml/3 tbsp *sumac*, to garnish
(optional)
rice, to serve

*1* Place the meat on a chopping board. Using a sharp knife remove any excess fat from the meat and cut the meat into strips, approximately 1cm/½in thick and 4cm/1½in long.

*2* Soak the saffron in 15ml/1 tbsp boiling water, pour into a small bowl and mix with the grated onion. Add to the meat and stir a few times so that the meat is coated thoroughly. Cover loosely with clear film and leave to marinate overnight in the fridge.

*3* Season the meat with salt and pepper and then thread on to flat skewers, aligning the strips in neat rows. Thread the tomatoes on to two separate skewers.

*4* Grill the kebabs and tomatoes over hot charcoal for 10–12 minutes, basting with butter and turning occasionally. Serve with rice, sprinkled with *sumac*, if you like.

---

# Shish Kebab

## INGREDIENTS

*Serves 4*
450g/1lb boned leg of lamb, cubed
1 large green pepper, seeded and cut into squares
1 large yellow pepper, seeded and cut into squares
8 baby onions, halved
225g/8oz button mushrooms
4 tomatoes, halved
15ml/1 tbsp melted butter
bulgur wheat, to serve

### For the marinade
45ml/3 tbsp olive oil
juice of 1 lemon
2 garlic cloves, crushed
1 large onion, grated
15ml/1 tbsp fresh oregano
salt and freshly ground black pepper

*1* First make the marinade: blend together the oil, lemon juice, garlic, onion, oregano and seasoning. Place the meat in a shallow dish and pour over the marinade.

*2* Cover with clear film and leave to marinate overnight in the fridge.

*3* Thread the cubes of lamb on to skewers, alternating with pieces of green and yellow pepper, onions and mushrooms. Thread the tomatoes on to separate skewers. Grill the kebabs and tomatoes over hot charcoal for 10–12 minutes basting with butter. Serve with bulgur wheat.

# Lebanese Kibbeh

The national dish of Syria and the Lebanon is *kibbeh*, a kind of meatball made from minced lamb and bulgur wheat. Raw *kibbeh* is the most widely eaten type, but this version is very popular too.

## INGREDIENTS

*Serves 6*
115g/4oz/¾ cup bulgur wheat
450g/1lb finely minced lean lamb
1 large onion, grated
15ml/1 tbsp melted butter
salt and freshly ground black pepper
sprigs of mint, to garnish
rice, to serve

**For the filling**
30ml/2 tbsp oil
1 onion, finely chopped
225g/8oz minced lamb or veal
50g/2oz/½ cup pine nuts
2.5ml/½ tsp ground allspice

**For the yogurt dip**
600ml/1 pint/2½ cups Greek yogurt
2–3 garlic cloves, crushed
15–30ml/1–2 tbsp chopped fresh mint

*1* Preheat the oven to 190°C/375°F/ Gas 5. Rinse the bulgur wheat in a sieve and squeeze out the excess moisture.

*2* Mix the lamb, onion and seasoning, kneading the mixture to make a thick paste. Add the bulgur wheat and blend together.

*3* To make the filling, heat the oil in a frying pan and fry the onion until golden. Add the lamb or veal and cook, stirring, until evenly browned and then add the pine nuts, allspice and salt and pepper.

*4* Oil a large baking dish and spread half of the meat and bulgur wheat mixture over the bottom. Spoon over the filling and top with a second layer of meat and bulgur wheat, pressing down firmly with the back of a spoon.

*5* Pour the melted butter over the top and then bake in the oven for 40–45 minutes until browned on top.

*6* Meanwhile make the yogurt dip: blend together the yogurt and garlic, spoon into a serving bowl and sprinkle with the chopped mint.

*7* Cut the cooked *kibbeh* into squares or rectangles and serve garnished with mint and accompanied by rice and the yogurt dip.

# Koftas in Tomato Sauce

There are many varieties of *koftas* in the Middle East. This is a popular version from Turkey.

## INGREDIENTS

*Serves 4*
350g/12oz minced lamb or beef
25g/1oz/½ cup fresh breadcrumbs
1 onion, grated
45ml/3 tbsp chopped fresh parsley
15ml/1 tbsp chopped fresh mint
5ml/1 tsp ground cumin
5ml/1 tsp ground turmeric
45ml/3 tbsp oil for frying
salt and freshly ground black pepper
egg noodles, to serve
mint leaves, to garnish

**For the tomato sauce**
15ml/1 tbsp oil
1 onion, chopped
400g/14oz can plum tomatoes
15ml/1 tbsp tomato purée
juice of ½ lemon
salt and freshly ground black pepper

---
COOK'S TIP
---

Instead of using either minced lamb or beef, use a mixture of the two, if you like.

*1* First make the tomato sauce: heat the oil in a large saucepan or flameproof casserole and fry the onion until golden. Stir in the canned tomatoes, tomato purée, lemon juice and seasoning, bring to the boil and then reduce the heat and simmer for about 10 minutes.

*2* Meanwhile, place the minced lamb or beef in a large bowl and mix in the breadcrumbs, grated onion, herbs and spices and a little salt and pepper.

*3* Knead the mixture by hand until thoroughly blended and then shape the mixture into walnut-size balls and place on a plate.

*4* Heat the oil in a frying pan and fry the meatballs, in batches if necessary, until evenly browned. Transfer them into the tomato sauce. Cover the pan and simmer very gently for about 30 minutes. Serve with noodles and garnish with mint leaves.

# Spiced Roast Lamb

This is a very tasty Turkish version of a roast dinner.

### INGREDIENTS

*Serves 6–8*
2.75kg/6lb leg of lamb
3–4 large garlic cloves, halved
60ml/4 tbsp olive oil
10ml/2 tsp paprika
10ml/2 tsp Dijon mustard
juice of 1 lemon
2.5ml/½ tsp dried thyme
2.5ml/½ tsp dried rosemary
2.5ml/½ tsp sugar
120ml/4fl oz/½ cup white wine
salt and freshly ground black pepper
fresh thyme, to garnish
rice and green salad, to serve

---
COOK'S TIP

This dish is equally delicious served with roast potatoes and vegetables. Leave the meat to rest for 15 minutes, before slicing.

---

1 Trim the fat from the lamb and make several incisions in the meat with a sharp knife. Press the garlic halves into the slits.

2 Blend together the olive oil, paprika, mustard, lemon juice, herbs, sugar and seasoning and rub this paste all over the meat. Place the joint in a shallow dish and allow to stand in a cool place for 1–2 hours.

3 Preheat the oven to 200°C/400°F/ Gas 6. Place the joint in a roasting tin, add the wine and cook for 20 minutes. Reduce the heat to 160°C/325°F/Gas 3 and cook for a further 2 hours, basting occasionally. Serve garnished with thyme and accompanied by rice and a salad.

# Roast Leg of Lamb with Saffron

### INGREDIENTS

*Serves 6–8*
2.75kg/6lb leg of lamb
4 garlic cloves, halved
60ml/4 tbsp olive oil
juice of 1 lemon
2–3 saffron strands, soaked in
   15ml/1 tbsp boiling water
5ml/1 tsp dried mixed herbs
450g/1lb potatoes
2 large onions
salt and freshly ground black pepper
fresh parsley, to garnish

1 Make several incisions in the meat and press the garlic halves into the slits. Blend the oil, lemon juice, saffron and herbs. Rub over the meat, then leave to marinate for 2 hours.

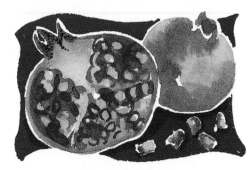

2 Preheat the oven to 180°C/350°F/ Gas 4. Peel the potatoes and cut them crossways into thick slices. Cut the onions into thick slices. Layer the potatoes and onions in a large roasting tin. Lift the lamb out of the marinade and place the marinated lamb on the top of the potatoes and onions, fat side up.

3 Pour any remaining marinade over the lamb and roast in the oven for 2 hours, basting occasionally. Remove the lamb from the oven, cover loosely with foil and leave in a warm place to rest for 10–15 minutes before carving. Serve garnished with fresh parsley.

# Lamb Couscous

Couscous can be served with all sorts of different stews. This is a popular dish from Morocco.

## INGREDIENTS

*Serves 4*
30ml/2 tbsp oil
1 large onion
450g/1lb lamb, cut into
    5cm/2in cubes
4 tomatoes, seeded and chopped
2 garlic cloves, halved
5ml/1 tsp ground ginger
5ml/1 tsp ground fennel seeds
5ml/1 tsp ground turmeric
2.5ml/½ tsp chilli sauce (optional)
50g/2oz/¼ cup canned chick-peas
225g/8oz/1¼ cups couscous
2 carrots, cut into small chunks
2 courgettes, cut into small chunks
4 new potatoes, halved
salt and freshly ground black pepper

---

### COOK'S TIP

Couscous can be successfully cooked using the microwave. Place the soaked couscous in a microwaveproof bowl, cover with clear film and microwave on medium for 5–6 minutes until tender.

---

*1* Heat 30ml/2 tbsp of the oil in a large saucepan and fry the onion for 4–5 minutes until softened. Add the meat and fry over a moderate heat until evenly browned all over.

*2* Place the tomatoes, garlic, ginger, fennel, turmeric and chilli sauce, if using, in a blender or food processor and blend to a smooth paste.

*3* Pour the tomato paste over the meat, add the chick-peas and 250ml/8fl oz/1 cup water and bring to the boil. Season with salt and pepper. Reduce the heat, cover the pan and simmer gently for about 45 minutes.

*4* Place the couscous in a large bowl and stir in the remaining oil and about 750ml/1¼ pints/3⅔ cups water, rubbing the couscous through your fingers to separate the grains. Set aside for about 15 minutes.

*5* Add the carrots, courgettes and potatoes to the stew and cook for a further 15–20 minutes.

*6* Place the couscous in a steamer or colander, making several deep holes in the surface with the handle of a wooden spoon. Set over the stew, cover tightly and steam for about 10 minutes, or until the couscous is tender and no longer grainy.

*7* Place the couscous on a large serving plate, make a dip in the centre and spoon over the lamb stew.

# Meat Dumplings with Yogurt

These Lebanese meat dumplings are braised in yogurt sauce, a speciality known as *Shish Barak*.

### INGREDIENTS

*Serves 4*
30ml/2 tbsp oil
1 large onion, chopped
60ml/4 tbsp pine nuts or
    chopped walnuts
450g/1lb minced lamb
25g/1oz/2 tbsp butter
3 garlic cloves, crushed
15ml/1 tbsp chopped fresh mint
salt and freshly ground black pepper
mint leaves, to garnish
rice and green salad, to serve

**For the dough**
5ml/1 tsp salt
225g/8oz/2 cups plain flour

**For the yogurt sauce**
2 litres/3½ pints/8 cups yogurt
1 egg, beaten
15ml/1 tbsp cornflour, blended with
    15ml/1 tbsp cold water
salt and white pepper

*1* First make the dough: mix the salt and the flour together and then stir in enough water for the dough to hold together. Leave to rest for 1 hour.

*2* Heat the oil in a large frying pan and fry the onion for 3–4 minutes until soft. Add the pine nuts or walnuts and fry until golden. Stir in the meat and cook until brown. Season, then remove the pan from the heat.

*3* Roll out the dough thinly on a floured board. Cut into small rounds 5–6cm/2–2½in in diameter. Place 5ml/1 tsp of filling on each one, fold the pastry over and firmly press the edges together. Bring the ends together to form a handle.

*4* Meanwhile, make the yogurt sauce: pour the yogurt into a saucepan and beat in the egg and cornflour mixture. Season with salt and white pepper and slowly bring to the boil, stirring constantly. Cook over a gentle heat until the sauce thickens and then carefully drop in the dumplings and simmer for about 20 minutes.

*5* Spoon the dumplings and sauce on to warmed serving plates. Melt the butter in a small frying pan and fry the garlic until golden. Stir in the mint, cook briefly and then pour over the dumplings. Garnish with mint leaves and serve with rice and a green salad.

# POULTRY AND GAME

*Poultry and game birds are popular throughout the Middle East and are prepared in a wide variety of ways. Grilled or barbecued, stewed with nuts or fruits, threaded on kebabs or stuffed and baked, poultry is an important feature of family meals and festivities. One of the most famous dishes – Khoreshe Fesenjan – consists of chicken portions simmered in an unusual and utterly delicious sauce that includes walnuts and pomegranate purée. Another version of* khoresh, *this time with aubergines and peppers, makes a colourful contribution to the table, while roast turkey, stuffed with prunes, dried apricots, nuts and rice, is irresistible.*

# Persian Chicken with Walnut Sauce

This distinctive dish, *Khoreshe Fesenjan*, is traditionally served on festive occasions in Iran.

## INGREDIENTS

*Serves 4*

30ml/2 tbsp oil
4 chicken pieces (leg or breast)
1 large onion, grated
250ml/8fl oz/1 cup water
115g/4oz/1 cup finely
  chopped walnuts
75ml/5 tbsp pomegranate purée
15ml/1 tbsp tomato purée
30ml/2 tbsp lemon juice
15ml/1 tbsp sugar
3–4 saffron strands dissolved in 15ml/
  1 tbsp boiling water
salt and freshly ground black pepper
Persian rice and salad leaves, to serve

*1* Heat 15ml/1 tbsp of the oil in a large saucepan or flameproof casserole and sauté the chicken pieces until golden brown. Add half of the grated onion and fry until slightly softened, then add the water and seasoning and bring to the boil. Cover the pan, reduce the heat and simmer for 15 minutes.

*2* Heat the remaining oil in a small saucepan or frying pan and fry the rest of the onion for 2–3 minutes until soft. Add the chopped walnuts and fry for a further 2–3 minutes over a low heat, stirring frequently and taking care that the walnuts do not burn.

*3* Stir in the pomegranate and tomato purées, lemon juice, sugar and the dissolved saffron. Season to taste and then simmer over a low heat for 5 minutes.

*4* Pour the walnut sauce over the chicken, ensuring all the pieces are well covered. Cover and simmer for 30–35 minutes until the meat is cooked and the oil of the walnuts has risen to the top.

*5* Serve at once with Persian rice and salad leaves.

---

COOK'S TIP

Pomegranate purée is available from Middle Eastern delicatessens.

---

# Chicken and Aubergine Khoresh

In Persian or Farsi this dish is known as *Khoreshe Bademjun*, *khoresh* meaning stew and *bademjun* meaning aubergines. It is often served on festive occasions and is believed to have been a favourite of kings.

## INGREDIENTS

*Serves 4*

30ml/2 tbsp oil
1 whole chicken or 4 large
  chicken pieces
1 large onion, chopped
2 garlic cloves, crushed
400g/14oz can chopped tomatoes
250ml/8fl oz/1 cup water
3 aubergines, sliced
3 peppers, preferably red, green and
  yellow, seeded and sliced
30ml/2 tbsp lemon juice
15ml/1 tbsp ground cinnamon
salt and freshly ground black pepper
Persian rice, to serve

*1* Heat 15ml/1 tbsp of the oil in a large saucepan or flameproof casserole and fry the chicken or chicken pieces on both sides for about 10 minutes. Add the onion and fry for a further 4–5 minutes, until the onion is golden brown.

*2* Add the garlic, the chopped tomatoes and their liquid, water and seasoning. Bring to the boil, then reduce the heat and simmer slowly, covered, for 10 minutes.

*3* Meanwhile, heat the remaining oil and fry the aubergines in batches until lightly golden. Transfer to a plate with a slotted spoon. Add the peppers to the pan and fry for a few minutes until slightly softened.

*4* Place the aubergines over the chicken or chicken pieces and then add the peppers. Sprinkle over the lemon juice and cinnamon, then cover and continue cooking over a low heat for about 45 minutes, or until the chicken is cooked.

*5* Transfer the chicken to a serving plate and spoon the aubergines and peppers around the edge. Reheat the sauce if necessary, adjust the seasoning and pour over the chicken. Serve the *khoresh* with Persian rice.

# Chicken Kebabs

Chicken kebabs are prepared in very much the same way all over the Middle East and are a great favourite everywhere. They are ideal for barbecues on hot summer evenings.

## INGREDIENTS

*Serves 6–8*
2 young chickens
1 large onion, grated
2 garlic cloves, crushed
120ml/4fl oz/½ cup olive oil
juice of 1 lemon
5ml/1 tsp paprika
2–3 saffron strands, soaked in
    15ml/1 tbsp boiling water
salt and freshly ground black pepper
naan or pitta bread, to serve

*1* Cut the chicken into small pieces, removing the bone if preferred, and place in a shallow bowl. Mix the onion, garlic, olive oil, lemon juice, paprika and saffron, and season with salt and pepper.

*2* Pour the marinade over the chicken, turning the chicken so that all the pieces are covered evenly. Cover the bowl loosely with clear film and leave in a cool place to marinate for at least 2 hours.

*3* Thread the chicken on to long, preferably metal, skewers. If barbecuing, once the coals are ready, cook for 10–15 minutes, turning occasionally. Or, if you prefer, cook under a moderately hot grill for about 10–15 minutes, turning occasionally.

*4* Serve with naan or pitta bread. Or you could remove boneless chicken from the skewers and serve it in pitta bread as a sandwich accompanied by a garlicky yogurt sauce.

# Baked Poussins

This dish is ideal for dinner parties. It is very easy to make and very tasty too. Allow ample time to make this recipe, however. The poussins should be allowed to marinate to make them extra delicious.

## INGREDIENTS

*Serves 4*
475ml/16fl oz/2 cups yogurt
60ml/4 tbsp olive oil
1 large onion, grated
2 garlic cloves, crushed
2.5ml/½ tsp paprika
2–3 saffron strands, soaked in
    15ml/1 tbsp boiling water
juice of 1 lemon
4 poussins, halved
salt and freshly ground black pepper
cos lettuce salad, to serve

*1* Blend together the yogurt, olive oil, onion, garlic, paprika, saffron and lemon juice, and season with salt and pepper.

*2* Place the poussin halves in a shallow dish, pour over the marinade and then cover and allow to marinate overnight in a cool place or for at least 4 hours in the fridge.

*3* Preheat the oven to 180°C/350°F/ Gas 4. Arrange the poussins in a greased ovenproof dish and bake in the oven for 30–45 minutes, basting frequently until cooked. Serve with cos lettuce salad.

> ——————— COOK'S TIP ———————
>
> The poussins can also be barbecued, for an authentic and even more delicious taste.

# Stuffed Spring Chickens

This dish is widely found in the Lebanon and Syria. The stuffing is a delicious blend of meat, nuts and rice and makes a great dinner party dish.

## INGREDIENTS

*Serves 6–8*
2 x 1kg/2¼lb chickens
15ml/1 tbsp butter
yogurt and salad, to serve

### For the stuffing
45ml/3 tbsp oil
1 onion, chopped
450g/1lb minced lamb
75g/3oz/¾ cup almonds, chopped
75g/3oz/¾ cup pine nuts
350g/12oz/2 cups cooked rice
salt and freshly ground black pepper

*1* Preheat the oven to 180°C/350°F/ Gas 4. Remove the giblets, if necessary, from the chickens and rinse the body cavities in cold water.

*2* Heat the oil in a large frying pan and sauté the onion until slightly softened. Add the minced lamb and cook over a moderate heat for 4–8 minutes until well browned, stirring frequently. Set aside.

*3* Heat a small pan over a moderate heat and dry fry the almonds and pine nuts for 2–3 minutes until golden, shaking the pan frequently.

*4* Mix together the meat mixture, almonds, pine nuts and cooked rice. Season with salt and pepper, and then spoon the mixture into the body cavities of the chickens. Rub the chickens all over with the butter.

*5* Place the chickens in a large roasting dish, cover with foil and bake in the oven for 45–60 minutes. After about 30 minutes, remove the foil and baste the chickens with the pan juices. Continue cooking without the foil until the chickens are cooked through and the meat juices run clear. Serve the chickens, cut into portions, with yogurt and a salad.

# Chicken and Olives

**INGREDIENTS**

*Serves 4*

30ml/2 tbsp olive oil
1.5kg/3–3½lb chicken
1 large onion, sliced
15ml/1 tbsp fresh root ginger,
  grated
3 garlic cloves, crushed
5ml/1 tsp paprika
250ml/8fl oz/1 cup chicken stock
2–3 saffron strands, soaked in
  15ml/1 tbsp boiling water
4–5 spring onions, chopped
15–20 black and green olives, pitted
juice of ½ lemon
salt and freshly ground black pepper

*1* Heat the oil in a large saucepan or flameproof casserole and sauté the chicken on both sides until golden.

*2* Add the onion, ginger, garlic, paprika, and seasoning and continue frying over a moderate heat, coating the chicken with the mixture.

*3* Add the chicken stock and saffron and bring to the boil. Cover and simmer gently for 45 minutes, or until the chicken is well done.

*4* Add the spring onions and cook for a further 15 minutes until the chicken is well cooked and the sauce is reduced to about 120ml/4fl oz/½ cup.

*6* Place the chicken on a large deep plate and pour over the sauce. Serve with rice and a mixed salad.

*5* Add the olives and lemon juice and cook for a further 5 minutes.

# Persian Chicken

## INGREDIENTS

*Serves 4*
15ml/1 tbsp oil
4 chicken pieces
1 large onion, chopped
3 garlic cloves, finely chopped
5ml/1 tsp ground cinnamon
2–3 saffron strands, soaked in
    15ml/1 tbsp boiling water
30ml/2 tbsp lemon juice
475ml/16fl oz/2 cups water
salt and freshly ground black pepper
Persian rice, yogurt and salad,
    to serve

*1* Heat the oil in a large saucepan or
flameproof casserole and sauté the
chicken pieces until golden.

*2* Remove the chicken pieces from
the pan or casserole. Add the onion
and fry gently over a moderate heat for
about 5 minutes, stirring frequently,
until softened and golden, then add the
garlic and fry briefly.

*3* Stir in the cinnamon, saffron and
lemon juice and seasoning. Return
the chicken to the pan, add the water
and bring to the boil. Reduce the heat,
cover and simmer for 30–45 minutes
until the chicken is cooked and the
sauce reduced to 120ml/4fl oz/½ cup.
Serve with rice, yogurt and salad.

# Stuffed Roast Turkey

## INGREDIENTS

*Serves 6–8*
5–6kg/12–14lb turkey
juice of 2 lemons
30ml/2 tbsp olive oil
roast potatoes and vegetables, to serve

**For the stuffing**
15ml/1 tbsp butter
1 large onion, chopped
200g/7oz/1¼ cups prunes, stoned
    and chopped
200g/7oz/1¼ cups dried apricots,
    soaked and chopped
50g/2oz/⅓ cup seedless raisins
    (optional)
175g/6oz/1½ cups chopped mixed
    nuts, such as walnuts, almonds, pine
    nuts and pistachios
400g/14oz/2 cups rice, cooked
5ml/1 tsp ground cinnamon
5ml/1 tsp ground turmeric
2–3 saffron strands, soaked in
    15ml/1 tbsp boiling water
salt and freshly ground black pepper

*1* Preheat the oven to 160°C/325°F/
Gas 3. Melt the butter in a large
saucepan or flameproof casserole and
sauté the onion for 3–4 minutes until
slightly softened. Add the chopped
prunes and apricots, and the raisins
if using, and continue frying for
2 minutes. Stir in the nuts and fry for a
further 2–3 minutes then add the rice,
spices and seasoning and blend well.

*2* Loosely stuff the neck cavity of the
turkey with the mixture, and
lightly sew the openings with strong
thread. Weigh the turkey in order to
calculate cooking times.

*3* Rub the bird with salt and pepper,
place in a large roasting tin and
roast in the oven for 20 minutes per
450g/1lb, basting frequently with
lemon juice and olive oil. Serve with
roast potatoes and cooked vegetables or
rice and salad, if you prefer.

---
COOK'S TIP

This spicy, fruit- and nut-stuffed roast
turkey makes an excellent alternative for a
festive meal and is delicious served with
either *Shirin Polo* (sweet rice), or the more
traditional roast potatoes and vegetables.

# FISH DISHES

*One of the finest ways of enjoying fish is to grill it over hot charcoal, a cooking method which is used to excellent effect all over the Middle East. Red mullet, salmon trout, sole and swordfish are popular varieties, along with cod, sardines, tuna and white fish. Salted and dried fish are Iranian specialities and are traditionally served with a special herb rice for Persian New Year. The world's finest caviar, beluga, comes from the Caspian Sea, which borders Iran to the north.*

# Prawns in Tomato Sauce

Prawns are popular everywhere in the Middle East. This delicious recipe is an easy way of making the most of them.

## Ingredients

*Serves 4*

30ml/2 tbsp oil
2 onions, finely chopped
2–3 garlic cloves, crushed
5–6 tomatoes, peeled and chopped
30ml/2 tbsp tomato purée
120ml/4fl oz/½ cup fish stock
   or water
2.5ml/½ tsp ground cumin
2.5ml/½ tsp ground cinnamon
450g/1lb raw, peeled Mediterranean
   prawns
juice of 1 lemon
salt and freshly ground black pepper
fresh parsley, to garnish
rice, to serve

*1* Heat the oil in a large frying pan or saucepan and fry the onions for 3–4 minutes until golden. Add the garlic, fry for about 1 minute, and then stir in the tomatoes.

*2* Blend the tomato purée with the stock or water and stir into the pan with the cumin, cinnamon and seasoning. Simmer, covered, over a low heat for 15 minutes, stirring occasionally. Do not allow to boil.

*3* Add the prawns and lemon juice and simmer the sauce for a further 10–15 minutes over a low to moderate heat until the prawns are cooked and the stock is reduced by about half.

*4* Serve with plain rice or in a decorative ring of Persian Rice, garnished with parsley.

# Swordfish Kebabs

Fish is most delicious when cooked over hot charcoal.

## Ingredients

*Serves 4–6*

900g/2lb swordfish steaks
45ml/3 tbsp olive oil
juice of ½ lemon
1 garlic clove, crushed
5ml/1 tsp paprika
3 tomatoes, quartered
2 onions, cut into wedges
salt and freshly ground black pepper
salad and pitta bread, to serve

---
COOK'S TIP

Almost any type of firm white fish can be used for this recipe.

---

*1* Cut the fish into large cubes and place in a dish.

*2* Blend together the oil, lemon juice, garlic, paprika and seasoning in a small mixing bowl and pour over the fish. Cover loosely with clear film and leave to marinate in a cool place for up to 2 hours.

*3* Thread the fish cubes on to skewers alternating with pieces of tomato and onion.

*4* Grill the kebabs over hot charcoal for 5–10 minutes, basting frequently with the remaining marinade and turning occasionally. Serve with salad and pitta bread.

# Tahini Baked Fish

This simple dish is a great favourite in many Arab countries, particularly Egypt, the Lebanon and Syria.

## INGREDIENTS

*Serves 6*

6 cod or haddock fillets
juice of 2 lemons
60ml/4 tbsp olive oil
2 large onions, chopped
250ml/8fl oz/1 cup tahini paste
1 garlic clove, crushed
45–60ml/3–4 tbsp water
salt and freshly ground black pepper
rice and salad, to serve

*1* Preheat the oven to 180°C/350°F/ Gas 4. Arrange the fish fillets in a shallow ovenproof dish, pour over 15ml/1 tbsp each of the lemon juice and olive oil and bake in the oven for 20 minutes.

*2* Meanwhile heat the remaining oil in a large frying pan and fry the onions for 6–8 minutes until well browned and almost crisp.

*3* Put the tahini paste, garlic and seasoning in a small bowl and slowly beat in the remaining lemon juice and water, a little at a time, until the sauce is light and creamy.

*4* Sprinkle the onions over the fish, pour over the tahini sauce and bake for a further 15 minutes, until the fish is cooked through and the sauce is bubbling. Serve the fish at once with rice and a salad.

# Baked Fish with Nuts

This speciality comes from Egypt and is as delicious as it is unusual.

**INGREDIENTS**

*Serves 4*
45ml/3 tbsp oil
4 small red mullet
1 large onion, finely chopped
75g/3oz/³/₄ cup hazelnuts, chopped
75g/3oz/³/₄ cup pine nuts
3–4 tomatoes, sliced
45–60ml/3–4 tbsp finely chopped
 fresh parsley
250ml/8fl oz/1 cup fish stock
salt and freshly ground black pepper
parsley sprigs, to garnish
new potatoes or rice, and vegetables or
 salad, to serve

*1* Preheat the oven to 190°C/375°F/ Gas 5. Heat 30ml/2 tbsp of the oil in a frying pan and fry the fish, two at a time, until crisp on both sides.

*2* Heat the remaining oil in a large saucepan or flameproof casserole and fry the onion for 3–4 minutes until golden. Add the chopped hazelnuts and pine nuts and stir fry for a few minutes.

*3* Stir in the tomatoes, cook for a few minutes and then add the parsley, seasoning and stock and simmer for 10–15 minutes, stirring occasionally.

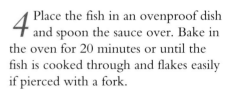

*4* Place the fish in an ovenproof dish and spoon the sauce over. Bake in the oven for 20 minutes or until the fish is cooked through and flakes easily if pierced with a fork.

*5* Serve the fish at once accompanied by new potatoes or rice, and vegetables or salad.

─── COOK'S TIP ───

Other small whole fish, such as snapper or trout, can be used for this recipe if mullet is unavailable.

# Fish with Herb Rice

## INGREDIENTS

*Serves 4*
2–3 saffron strands
2 egg yolks
1 garlic clove, crushed
4 salmon trout steaks
oil, for deep frying
salt and freshly ground black pepper
Rice with Fresh Herbs and green salad,
    to serve

*1* Soak the saffron in 15ml/1 tbsp boiling water and then beat the mixture into the egg yolks. Season with garlic, salt and pepper.

*2* Place the fish steaks in a shallow dish and coat with the egg mixture. Cover with clear film and marinate for up to 1 hour.

*3* Heat the oil in a deep fryer until it's very hot and then fry the fish, one steak at a time, for about 10 minutes until golden brown. Drain each one on kitchen paper. Serve with Rice with Fresh Herbs, lemon wedges and a green salad.

---
COOK'S TIP

Any type of fish can be used in this recipe. Try a combination of plain and smoked for a delicious change, such as smoked and unsmoked cod or haddock.

---

# Pan-fried Sardines

This delicious fish recipe is a favourite in many Arab countries.

## INGREDIENTS

*Serves 4*
10g/ 1⁄4oz fresh parsley
3–4 garlic cloves, crushed
8–12 sardines, prepared
30ml/2 tbsp lemon juice
50g/2oz/1⁄2 cup plain flour
2.5ml/1⁄2 tsp ground cumin
60ml/4 tbsp vegetable oil
salt and freshly ground black pepper
naan bread and salad, to serve

---
COOK'S TIP

If you don't have a garlic crusher, crush the garlic using the flat-side of a large knife blade instead.

---

*1* Finely chop the parsley and mix in a small bowl with the garlic.

*2* Pat the parsley and garlic mixture all over the outsides and insides of the sardines. Sprinkle them with the lemon juice and set aside, covered, in a cool place for about 2 hours to absorb the flavours.

*3* Place the flour on a large plate and season with cumin, salt and pepper. Roll the sardines in the flour, taking care to coat each fish thoroughly.

*4* Heat the oil in a large frying pan and fry the fish in batches for 5 minutes on each side until crisp. Keep warm in the oven while cooking the remaining fish and then serve with naan bread and salad.

# Fish with Rice

This Arabic fish dish, *Sayadieh,* is very popular in the Lebanon.

## INGREDIENTS

*Serves 4–6*
juice of 1 lemon
45ml/3 tbsp oil
900g/2lb cod steaks
4 large onions, chopped
5ml/1 tsp ground cumin
2–3 saffron strands
1 litre/1¾ pints/4 cups fish stock
450g/1lb/2⅔ cups basmati or other
   long grain rice
50g/2oz/½ cup pine nuts, lightly toasted
salt and freshly ground black pepper
fresh parsley, to garnish

---
COOK'S TIP
---

Take care when cooking the rice that the saucepan does not boil dry. Check it occasionally and add more stock or water if it becomes necessary.

*1* Blend together the lemon juice and 15ml/1 tbsp of the oil in a shallow dish. Add the fish steaks, turning to coat thoroughly, then cover and leave to marinate for 30 minutes.

*2* Heat the remaining oil in a large saucepan or flameproof casserole and fry the onions for 5–6 minutes until golden, stirring occasionally.

*3* Drain the fish, reserving the marinade, and add to the pan. Fry for 1–2 minutes each side until lightly golden, then add the cumin, saffron strands and a little salt and pepper.

*4* Pour in the fish stock and the reserved marinade, bring to the boil and then simmer very gently over a low heat for 5–10 minutes until the fish is nearly done.

*5* Transfer the fish to a plate and add the rice to the stock. Bring to the boil and then reduce the heat and simmer very gently over a low heat for 15 minutes until nearly all the stock has been absorbed.

*6* Arrange the fish on the rice and cover. Steam over a low heat for a further 15–20 minutes.

*7* Transfer the fish to a plate, then spoon the rice on to a large flat dish and arrange the fish on top. Sprinkle with toasted pine nuts and garnish with fresh parsley.

# *Turkish Cold Fish*

Cold fish dishes are much appreciated in the Middle East and for good reason – they are delicious! This particular version from Turkey can be made using mackerel if preferred.

## INGREDIENTS

*Serves 4*

60ml/4 tbsp olive oil
900g/2lb red mullet or snapper
2 onions, sliced
1 green pepper, seeded and sliced
1 red pepper, seeded and sliced
3 garlic cloves, crushed
15ml/1 tbsp tomato purée
50ml/2fl oz/¼ cup fish stock
   or water
5–6 tomatoes, peeled and sliced or
   400g/14oz can tomatoes
30ml/2 tbsp chopped fresh parsley
30ml/2 tbsp lemon juice
5ml/1 tsp paprika
15–20 green and black olives
salt and freshly ground black pepper
bread and salad, to serve

*1* Heat 30ml/2 tbsp of the oil in a large roasting tin or frying pan and fry the fish on both sides until golden brown. Remove from the tin or pan, cover and keep warm.

─────── COOK'S TIP ───────

One large fish looks spectacular, but it is tricky to both cook and serve. If you prefer, buy four smaller fish and cook for a shorter time, until just tender and cooked through but not overdone.

*2* Heat the remaining oil in the tin or pan and fry the onion for 2–3 minutes until slightly softened. Add the green and red peppers and continue cooking for 3–4 minutes, stirring occasionally, then add the garlic and stir fry for a further minute.

*3* Blend the tomato purée with the fish stock or water and stir into the pan with the tomatoes, parsley, lemon juice, paprika and seasoning. Simmer gently without boiling for 15 minutes, stirring occasionally.

*4* Return the fish to the tin or pan and cover with the sauce. Cook for 10 minutes then add the olives and cook for a further 5 minutes or until just cooked through.

*5* Transfer the fish to a serving dish and pour the sauce over the top. Allow to cool, then cover and chill until completely cold. Serve cold with bread and salad.

# RICE
# AND
# VEGETABLES

*Rice in some form is served at almost every Middle Eastern meal, from plain boiled and buttered Iranian* Chelo *to elaborate combinations of rice, meat, vegetables and nuts.* Polo *resembles a pilau, in that the accompaniments are mixed in and cooked with the rice. Rice is very easy to prepare and the Persian method gives particularly good results. When rice is cooked this way, a crisp golden crust forms at the bottom; this is the* tahdiq, *regarded by many as the best part of the rice. Stuffed vegetables, salads and a delicious soufflé round off this chapter.*

# Persian Rice

Plain rice in Iran is called *Chelo*. The rice is soaked in salted water before cooking. Don't skimp on this process – the longer it is soaked, the better the flavour of the finished rice.

**INGREDIENTS**

*Serves 4*
350g/12oz/scant 2 cups long
  grain rice
about 20ml/4 tsp salt
45ml/3 tbsp melted butter
2–3 saffron strands, soaked in 15ml/
  1 tbsp boiling water (optional)

*1* Soak the rice in lukewarm water, salted with 15ml/1 tbsp salt for a minimum of two hours.

*2* When the rice has soaked, and you are ready to cook, fill a non-stick pan with fresh water, add a little salt and bring to the boil.

*3* Drain the rice and stir into the boiling water. Boil for 5 minutes, then reduce the heat and simmer for about 10 minutes until half cooked. Drain and rinse in lukewarm water. Wash and dry the pan.

*4* Heat 30ml/2 tbsp of the melted butter in the saucepan. Make sure you do not over cook it or it will burn. Add about 15ml/1 tbsp water and stir in the rice. Cook the rice over a very low heat for 10 minutes then pour over the remaining butter.

*5* Cover the pan with a clean dish towel and secure with a tightly fitting lid, lifting the corners of the cloth back over the lid.

*6* Steam the rice for 30–40 minutes. The cloth will absorb the excess steam and will turn the bottom of the rice into a crisp, golden crust called *tahdig*. This is regarded by many as the best part of the rice. To serve, if you like, mix 30–45ml/2–3 tbsp of the rice with the saffron water and sprinkle over the top of the rice.

# Plain Rice

This is a simplified and quicker version of Persian Rice (*Chelo*).

**INGREDIENTS**

*Serves 4*
750ml/1¼ pints/3⅔ cups water
5ml/1 tsp salt
350g/12oz/scant 2 cups basmati rice
1½oz/40g/3 tbsp butter

*1* Place the water and salt in a non-stick saucepan and pour in the rice. Set aside to soak for at least 30 minutes and for up to 2 hours.

*2* Bring the water and rice to the boil, then reduce the heat and simmer for 10–15 minutes until the water is absorbed.

*3* Add the butter to the rice, cover the pan with a tight-fitting lid and steam over a very low heat for about 30 minutes. Serve with *Khoresh*, or any other meat dish.

# Sweet and Sour Rice

*Zereshk Polo* is flavoured with fruit and spices and is commonly served with chicken dishes.

## INGREDIENTS

*Serves 4*

50g/2oz *zereshk*
45ml/3 tbsp melted butter
50g/2oz/⅓ cup raisins
30ml/2 tbsp sugar
5ml/1 tsp ground cinnamon
5ml/1 tsp ground cumin
350g/12oz/scant 2 cups basmati rice,
   soaked in salted water for 2 hours
2–3 saffron strands, soaked in 15ml/
   1 tbsp boiling water
salt

*1* Thoroughly wash the *zereshk* in cold water at least 4–5 times to rinse off any bits of grit.

*2* Heat 15ml/1 tbsp of the butter in a small frying pan and stir fry the raisins for 1–2 minutes.

*3* Add the *zereshk*, fry for a few seconds and then add the sugar, and half of the cinnamon and cumin. Cook briefly and then set aside.

*4* Drain the rice and then boil in salted water for 5 minutes, reduce the heat and simmer for 10 minutes until half cooked.

*5* Drain and rinse in lukewarm water and wash and dry the pan. Heat half of the remaining butter in the pan, add 15ml/1 tbsp water and stir in half of the rice.

*6* Sprinkle with half of the raisin and *zereshk* mixture and top with all but 45ml/3 tbsp of the rice. Sprinkle over the remaining raisin mixture.

*7* Blend the reserved rice with the remaining cinnamon and cumin and scatter over the top of the rice mixture. Dribble the remaining butter over and then cover the pan with a clean dish towel and secure with a tightly fitting lid, lifting the corners of the cloth back over the lid. Steam the rice over a very low heat for about 30–40 minutes.

*8* Just before serving, mix 45ml/ 3 tbsp of the rice with the saffron water. Spoon the rice on to a large flat serving dish and scatter the saffron rice over the top to decorate.

--- COOK'S TIP ---

*Zereshk* are very small dried berries that are delicious mixed with rice. They are available from most Persian and Middle Eastern food stores.

# Rice with Dill and Broad Beans

This is another favourite rice dish from Iran where it is called *Baghali Polo.*

## INGREDIENTS

### Serves 4

275g/10oz/1½ cups basmati rice,
   soaked in salted water for 3 hours
45ml/3 tbsp melted butter
175g/6oz/1½ cups broad beans, fresh
   or frozen
90ml/6 tbsp finely chopped fresh dill
5ml/1 tsp ground cinnamon
5ml/1 tsp ground cumin
2–3 saffron strands, soaked in
   15ml/1 tbsp boiling water
salt

*1* Drain the rice and then boil in salted water for 5 minutes. Reduce the heat and simmer very gently for 10 minutes until half cooked. Drain and rinse in lukewarm water.

*2* Put 15ml/1 tbsp of the melted butter in a non-stick saucepan and then add enough rice to cover the bottom of the pan. Add a quarter of the broad beans and a little of the dill.

*3* Add another layer of rice, followed by a layer of broad beans and dill and continue making layers until all the beans and dill are used, finishing with a layer of rice.

*4* Cook over a gentle heat for 10 minutes. Pour the remaining melted butter over the rice.

*5* Sprinkle the cinnamon and cumin evenly over the top of the rice. Cover the pan with a clean dish towel and secure with a tightly fitting lid, lifting the corners of the cloth back over the lid, and then steam over a very low heat for 30–45 minutes.

*6* Mix 45ml/3 tbsp of the rice with the saffron water. Spoon the remaining rice on to a large serving plate and scatter over the saffron rice to decorate. Serve with either a lamb or chicken dish.

# Sweet Rice

In Iran, sweet rice, *Shirin Polo,* is always served at wedding banquets and on other traditional special occasions.

## INGREDIENTS

### Serves 8–10

3 oranges
90ml/6 tbsp sugar
45ml/3 tbsp melted butter
5–6 carrots, cut into julienne strips
50g/2oz/½ cup mixed chopped
   pistachios, almonds and pine nuts
675g/1½ lb/3½ cups basmati rice,
   soaked in salted water for 2 hours
2–3 saffron strands, soaked in
   15ml/1 tbsp boiling water
salt

---
COOK'S TIP
---

Take care to cook this rice over a very low heat as it can burn easily owing to the sugar in the carrots.

1 Cut the peel from the oranges in wide strips using a potato peeler, and cut the peel into thin shreds.

2 Place the strips of peel in a saucepan with enough water to cover and bring to the boil. Simmer for a few minutes, drain and repeat this process until you have removed the bitter flavour of the peel.

3 Place the peel back in the pan with 45ml/3 tbsp of the sugar and 60ml/4 tbsp water. Bring to the boil and then simmer until the water is reduced by half. Set aside.

4 Heat 15ml/1 tbsp of the butter in a pan and fry the carrots for 2–3 minutes. Add the remaining sugar and 60ml/4 tbsp water and simmer for 10 minutes until almost evaporated.

5 Stir the carrots and half of the nuts into the orange peel and set aside. Drain the rice, boil in salted water for 5 minutes, then reduce the heat and simmer very gently for 10 minutes until half cooked. Drain and rinse.

6 Heat 15ml/1 tbsp of the remaining butter in the pan and add 45ml/3 tbsp water. Fork a little of the rice into the pan and spoon on some of the orange mixture. Make layers until all the mixture has been used.

7 Cook gently for 10 minutes. Pour over the remaining butter and cover with a clean dish towel. Secure the lid and steam for 30–45 minutes. Serve garnished with the remaining nuts and the saffron water.

# Rice with Fresh Herbs

## INGREDIENTS

### Serves 4

350g/12oz/scant 2 cups basmati
   rice, soaked in salted water for
   2 hours
30ml/2 tbsp finely chopped
   fresh parsley
30ml/2 tbsp finely chopped
   fresh coriander
30ml/2 tbsp finely chopped
   fresh chives
15ml/1 tbsp finely chopped fresh dill
3–4 spring onions, finely chopped
60ml/4 tbsp butter
5ml/1 tsp ground cinnamon
2–3 saffron strands, soaked in
   15ml/1 tbsp boiling water
salt

1 Drain the rice, and then boil in salted water for 5 minutes, reduce the heat and simmer for 10 minutes.

2 Stir in the herbs and spring onions and mix well with a fork. Simmer for a few minutes more, then drain but do not rinse. Wash and dry the pan.

3 Heat half of the butter in the pan, add 15ml/1 tbsp water, then stir in the rice. Cook over a very low heat for 10 minutes, then test to see if it is half cooked. Add the remaining butter, the cinnamon and saffron water and cover the pan with a clean dish towel. Secure with a tight-fitting lid, and steam over a very low heat for 30–40 minutes.

# French Beans, Rice and Beef

## INGREDIENTS

*Serves 4*

25g/1oz/2 tbsp butter or margarine
1 large onion, chopped
450g/1lb stewing beef, cubed
2 garlic cloves, crushed
5ml/1 tsp ground cinnamon
5ml/1 tsp ground cumin powder
5ml/1 tsp ground turmeric
450g/1lb tomatoes, chopped
30ml/2 tbsp tomato purée
350ml/12fl oz/1½ cups water
350g/12oz French beans
salt and freshly ground black pepper

## For the rice

275g/10oz/1½ cups basmati rice,
   soaked in salted water for 2 hours
1.75 litres/3 pints/7½ cups water
45ml/3 tbsp melted butter
2–3 saffron strands, soaked in 15ml/
   1 tbsp boiling water
salt

*1* Melt the butter or margarine in a large saucepan or flameproof casserole and fry the onion until golden. Add the meat and fry until evenly brown, and then add the garlic, spices, tomatoes, tomato purée and water. Season with salt and pepper. Bring to the boil, then reduce the heat and simmer over a low heat for about 30 minutes.

*2* Cut the French beans into pieces and add to the meat.

*3* Continue cooking the beans for a further 15 minutes until the meat is tender and most of the meat juices have evaporated.

*4* Meanwhile, prepare the rice. Drain and then boil the rice in the salted water for 5 minutes, reduce the heat and simmer very gently for about 10 minutes until half cooked. Drain and rinse the rice in warm water. Wash and dry the pan.

*5* Heat 15ml/1 tbsp of the melted butter in the pan and stir in about a third of the rice.

*6* Spoon half of the meat mixture over the rice, add a layer of rice, the remaining meat and finish with a layer of rice.

*7* Pour the remaining melted butter over the rice and cover the pan with a clean dish towel. Secure with the lid and then steam for 30–45 minutes over a low heat.

*8* Take 45ml/3 tbsp rice and mix with the saffron water. Serve the rice on a large flat dish and sprinkle the saffron rice on top.

# Yogurt Chicken and Rice

This rice dish, *Tah Chin*, is very unusual and tastes superb.

## INGREDIENTS

*Serves 6*

40g/1½ oz/3 tbsp butter
1.5kg/3–3½ lb chicken
1 large onion, chopped
250ml/8fl oz/1 cup chicken stock
2 eggs
475ml/16fl oz/2 cups natural yogurt
2–3 saffron strands, dissolved in
    15ml/1 tbsp boiling water
5ml/1 tsp ground cinnamon
450g/1lb/2 cups basmati rice
75g/3oz *zereshk*
salt and freshly ground black pepper
herb salad, to serve

*1* Melt 25g/1oz/2 tbsp of the butter and fry the chicken and onion for 4–5 minutes until the onion is softened and the chicken browned.

*2* Add the chicken stock and salt and pepper, bring to the boil and then reduce the heat and simmer for about 45 minutes, or until the chicken is cooked and the stock reduced by half.

*3* Skin and bone the chicken. Cut the flesh into large pieces and place in a large bowl. Reserve the stock.

---
COOK'S TIP
---

If you prefer, use boned chicken breasts or thighs instead of a whole chicken. These are available from most supermarkets.

*4* Beat the eggs and blend with the yogurt. Add the saffron water and cinnamon and season with salt and pepper. Pour over the chicken and leave to marinate for up to 2 hours.

*5* Drain the rice and then boil in salted water for 5 minutes, reduce the heat and simmer very gently for 10 minutes until half cooked. Drain and rinse in lukewarm water.

*6* Transfer the chicken from the yogurt mixture to a dish and mix half the rice into the yogurt.

*7* Preheat the oven to 160°C/325°F/Gas 3 and grease a large 10cm/4in deep ovenproof dish.

*8* Place the rice and yogurt mixture in the bottom of the dish, arrange the chicken pieces in a layer on top and then add the plain rice. Sprinkle with the *zereshk*.

*9* Mix the remaining butter with the chicken stock and pour over the rice. Cover tightly with foil and cook in the oven for 35–45 minutes.

*10* Leave the dish to cool for a few minutes. Place on a cold, damp cloth which will help lift the rice from the bottom of the dish, then run a knife around the edges of the dish. Place a large flat plate over the dish and turn out. You should have a rice "cake" which can be cut into wedges. Serve hot with a herb salad.

# Aubergine Bake

Aubergines are extremely popular all over the Middle East. This particular dish, *Kuku Bademjan*, comes from Iran.

## INGREDIENTS

*Serves 4*

60ml/4 tbsp oil
1 onion, finely chopped
3–4 garlic cloves, crushed
4 aubergines, cut into quarters
6 eggs
2–3 saffron strands, soaked in 15ml/
  1 tbsp boiling water
5ml/1 tsp paprika
salt and freshly ground black pepper
chopped fresh parsley, to garnish
bread and salad, to serve

*1* Preheat the oven to 180°C/350°F/ Gas 4. Heat 30ml/2 tbsp of the oil in a frying pan and fry the onion until golden. Add the garlic, fry for about 2 minutes and then add the aubergines and cook for 10–12 minutes until soft and golden brown. Cool and then chop the aubergines.

*2* Beat the eggs in a large bowl and stir in the aubergine mixture, saffron water, paprika and seasoning. Place the remaining oil in a deep ovenproof dish. Heat in the oven for a few minutes, then add the egg and aubergine mixture. Bake for 30–40 minutes until set. Garnish with parsley and serve with bread and salad.

# Turkish-style Vegetable Casserole

## INGREDIENTS

*Serves 4*

60ml/4 tbsp olive oil
1 large onion, chopped
2 aubergines, cut into small cubes
4 courgettes, cut into small chunks
4–5 okra, soaked in vinegar for
  30 minutes, cut into short lengths
1 green pepper, seeded and chopped
1 red or yellow pepper, seeded
  and chopped
115g/4oz/1 cup fresh or frozen peas
115g/4oz French beans
450g/1lb new potatoes, cubed
2.5ml/½ tsp ground cinnamon
2.5ml/½ tsp ground cumin
5ml/1 tsp paprika
4–5 tomatoes, skinned
400g/14oz can chopped tomatoes
30ml/2 tbsp chopped fresh parsley
3–4 garlic cloves, crushed
350ml/12fl oz/1½ cups vegetable stock
salt and freshly ground black pepper
black olives, to garnish

*1* Preheat the oven to 190°C/375°F/ Gas 5. Heat 45ml/3 tbsp of the oil in a heavy-based pan and fry the onion until golden. Add the aubergines, sauté for about 3 minutes and then add the courgettes, okra, green and red pepper, peas, beans and potatoes, together with the spices and seasoning. Cook for a further 3 minutes, stirring all the time. Transfer to a shallow ovenproof dish.

*2* Chop and seed the fresh tomatoes and mix with the canned tomatoes, parsley, garlic and the remaining olive oil in a bowl.

*3* Pour the stock over the vegetables and then spoon over the tomato mixture. Cover and cook in the oven for 45–60 minutes. Serve, garnished with black olives.

# Baked Stuffed Aubergines

The name of this famous Turkish *mezze* dish, *Imam Bayaldi*, literally means, "the Imam fainted" – perhaps with pleasure at the deliciousness of the dish.

## INGREDIENTS

*Serves 6*
3 aubergines
60ml/4 tbsp olive oil
1 large onion, chopped
1 small red pepper, seeded and diced
1 small green pepper, seeded and diced
3 garlic cloves, crushed
5–6 tomatoes, skinned and chopped
30ml/2 tbsp chopped fresh parsley
about 250ml/8fl oz/1 cup
    boiling water
15ml/1 tbsp lemon juice
salt and freshly ground black pepper
chopped fresh parsley, to garnish
bread, salad and yogurt dip, to serve

---
COOK'S TIP
---

This flavourful dish can be made in advance and is ideal for a buffet table.

*1* Preheat the oven to 190°C/375°F/ Gas 5. Cut the aubergines in half lengthways and scoop out the flesh, reserving the shells.

*2* Heat 30ml/2 tbsp of the olive oil and fry the onion and peppers for 5–6 minutes until both are slightly softened but not too tender.

*3* Add the garlic and continue to cook for a further 2 minutes then stir in the tomatoes, parsley and aubergine flesh. Season and then stir well and fry over a moderate heat for 2–3 minutes.

*4* Heat the remaining oil in a separate pan and fry the aubergine shells, two at a time, on both sides.

*5* Stuff the shells with the sautéed vegetables. Arrange the aubergines closely together in an ovenproof dish and pour enough boiling water around the aubergines to come halfway up their sides.

*6* Cover with foil and bake in the oven for 45–60 minutes until the aubergines are tender and most of the liquid has been absorbed.

*7* Place a half aubergine on each serving plate and sprinkle with a little lemon juice. Serve the aubergines hot or cold, garnished with parsley and accompanied by bread, salad and a yogurt dip.

# Spinach Pie

This Turkish dish, *Fatayer*, makes a healthy vegetarian dish.

## INGREDIENTS

*Serves 6*

900g/2lb fresh spinach, chopped
25g/1oz/2 tbsp butter or margarine
2 onions, chopped
2 garlic cloves, crushed
275g/10oz feta, crumbled
115g/4oz/¾ cup pine nuts
5 eggs, beaten
2 saffron strands, soaked in 10ml/
    2 tbsp boiling water
5ml/1 tsp paprika
1.5ml/¼ tsp ground cumin
1.5ml/¼ tsp ground cinnamon
14 sheets filo pastry
about 60ml/4 tbsp olive oil
salt and freshly ground black pepper
lettuce, to serve

*1* Place the spinach in a large colander, sprinkle with a little salt, rub into the leaves and leave for 30 minutes to drain the excess liquid.

*2* Preheat the oven to 180°C/350°F/ Gas 4. Melt the butter or margarine in a large pan and fry the onions until golden. Add the garlic, cheese and nuts. Remove from the heat and stir in the eggs, spinach, saffron and spices. Season with salt and pepper and mix well.

---

COOK'S TIP

Cheddar, Parmesan or any hard cheese can be added to this dish as well as the feta.

---

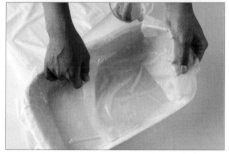

*3* Grease a large rectangular baking dish. Take seven of the sheets of filo and brush one side with a little olive oil. Place on the bottom of the dish, overlapping the sides.

*4* Spoon all of the spinach mixture over the pastry and carefully dribble 30ml/2 tbsp of the remaining olive oil over the top.

*5* Fold the overlapping pastry over the filling. Cut the remaining pastry sheets to the dish size and brush each one with more olive oil. Arrange on top of the filling.

*6* Brush with water to prevent curling and then bake in the oven for about 30 minutes, until the pastry is golden brown. Serve with the lettuce.

# Tabbouleh

This classic Lebanese salad has become very popular in other countries. It makes an ideal substitute for a rice dish on a buffet table and is excellent served with cold sliced lamb.

### INGREDIENTS

*Serves 4*
175g/6oz/1 cup fine
  bulgur wheat
juice of 1 lemon
45ml/3 tbsp olive oil
40g/1½oz fresh parsley, finely
  chopped
45ml/3 tbsp fresh mint, chopped
4–5 spring onions, chopped
1 green pepper, seeded and sliced
salt and freshly ground black pepper
2 large tomatoes, diced, and black

*1* Put the bulgur wheat in a bowl. Add enough cold water to cover the wheat and let it stand for at least 30 minutes and up to 2 hours.

*2* Drain and squeeze with your hands to remove excess water. The bulgur wheat will swell to double the size. Spread on kitchen paper to dry the bulgur wheat completely.

*3* Place the bulgur wheat in a large bowl, add the lemon juice, the oil and a little salt and pepper. Allow to stand for 1–2 hours if possible, in order for the flavours to develop.

*4* Add the chopped parsley, mint, spring onions and pepper and mix well. Garnish with diced tomatoes and olives and serve.

# Yogurt with Cucumber

### INGREDIENTS

*Serves 4–6*
½ cucumber
1 small onion
2 garlic cloves
10g/¼ oz fresh parsley
475ml/16fl oz/2 cups natural
  yogurt
1.5ml/¼ tsp paprika
salt and white pepper
mint leaves, to garnish

*1* Finely chop the cucumber and onion, crush the garlic and finely chop the parsley.

---
COOK'S TIP

It's not traditional, but other herbs, such as mint or chives, would be equally good in this dish.

---

*2* Lightly beat the yogurt and then add the cucumber, onion, garlic and parsley and season with salt and pepper to taste.

*3* Sprinkle with a little paprika and chill for at least 1 hour. Garnish with mint leaves and serve with warm pitta bread or as an accompaniment to meat, poultry and rice dishes.

# Turkish Salad

This classic salad is a wonderful combination of textures and flavours. The saltiness of the cheese is perfectly balanced by the refreshing salad vegetables.

## INGREDIENTS

*Serves 4*
1 cos lettuce heart
1 green pepper
1 red pepper
½ cucumber
4 tomatoes
1 red onion
225g/8oz feta cheese, crumbled
black olives, to garnish

### For the dressing
45ml/3 tbsp olive oil
45ml/3 tbsp lemon juice
1 garlic clove, crushed
15ml/1 tbsp chopped fresh parsley
15ml/1 tbsp chopped fresh mint
salt and freshly ground black pepper

*1* Chop the lettuce into bite-size pieces. Seed the peppers, remove the cores and cut the flesh into thin strips. Chop the cucumber and slice or chop the tomatoes. Cut the onion in half, then slice finely.

*2* Place the chopped lettuce, peppers, cucumber, tomatoes and onion in a large bowl. Scatter the feta over the top and toss together lightly.

*3* To make the dressing: blend together the olive oil, lemon juice and garlic in a small bowl. Stir in the parsley and mint and season with salt and pepper to taste.

*4* Pour the dressing over the salad, toss lightly and serve garnished with a handful of black olives.

# Persian Salad

This very simple salad can be served with pretty well any Persian dish – don't add the dressing until just before you are ready to serve.

## INGREDIENTS

*Serves 4*
4 tomatoes
½ cucumber
1 onion
1 cos lettuce heart

### For the dressing
30ml/2 tbsp olive oil
juice of 1 lemon
1 garlic clove, crushed
salt and freshly ground black pepper

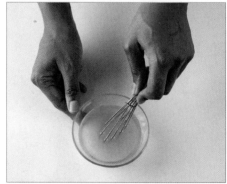

*1* Cut the tomatoes and cucumber into small cubes. Finely chop the onion and tear the lettuce into pieces.

*2* Place the tomatoes, cucumber, onion and lettuce in a large salad bowl and mix lightly together.

*3* To make the dressing, pour the olive oil into a small bowl. Add the lemon juice, garlic and seasoning and blend together well. Pour over the salad and toss lightly to mix. Sprinkle with black pepper and serve with meat or rice dishes.

# DESSERTS

*The most popular dessert in the Middle East is
fruit. The cornucopia includes melons of every
type, pomegranates, figs, cherries, grapes, apricots
and peaches, served simply or as a refreshing salad
scented with rose-water. Rich treats like Baklava,
Coconut Halva, and Almond Fingers are reserved
for special occasions or kept for callers – both
invited and unexpected. Traditional hospitality
demands that everyone who visits a Middle
Eastern home is offered food, so sweetmeats
are usually baked in sufficient quantity
to ensure that no guest ever goes hungry.*

# Persian Melon

Called *Paludeh Garmac*, this is a typical Persian dessert, using delicious, sweet fresh fruits flavoured with rose-water and a hint of aromatic mint.

## INGREDIENTS

*Serves 4*

2 small melons
225g/8oz/1 cup strawberries, sliced
3 peaches, peeled and cut into
    small cubes
1 bunch of seedless grapes (green or red)
30ml/2 tbsp caster sugar
15ml/1 tbsp rose-water
15ml/1 tbsp lemon juice
crushed ice (optional)
4 sprigs of mint, to decorate

*1* Carefully cut the melons in half and remove the seeds. Scoop out the flesh with a melon baller, making sure not to damage the skin. Reserve the melon shells. Alternatively, if you don't have a melon baller, scoop out the flesh using a large spoon and cut into bite-size pieces.

*2* Reserve four strawberries and slice the others. Place in a bowl with the melon balls, the peaches, grapes, sugar, rose-water and lemon juice.

*3* Pile the fruit into the melon shells and chill in the fridge for 2 hours.

*4* To serve, sprinkle with crushed ice, decorating each melon with a whole strawberry and a sprig of mint.

---

COOK'S TIP

To peel peaches, cover with boiling water and leave to stand for a couple of minutes. Cool under cold water before peeling.

# Oranges in Syrup

This is a favourite classic dessert. It is light and simple-to-make, refreshing and delicious.

## INGREDIENTS

*Serves 4*

4 oranges
600ml/1 pint/2½ cups water
350g/12oz/1½ cups sugar
30ml/2 tbsp lemon juice
30ml/2 tbsp orange blossom water or rose-water
50g/2oz/½ cup pistachio nuts, shelled and chopped

—— COOK'S TIP ——

A perfect dessert to serve after a heavy main course dish. Almonds could be substituted for the pistachio nuts, if you like.

*1* Peel the oranges with a potato peeler down to the pith.

*2* Cut the orange peel into fine strips and boil in water several times to remove the bitterness. Drain and set aside until required.

*3* Place the water, sugar and lemon juice in a saucepan. Bring to the boil and then add the orange peel and simmer until the syrup thickens. Add the orange blossom or rose-water, stir and leave to cool.

*4* Completely peel the pith from the oranges and cut them into thick slices. Arrange in a shallow serving dish and pour over the syrup. Chill for about 1–2 hours and then decorate with pistachio nuts and serve.

# Apple Froth

This is another very popular dessert. It is easy to make and is perfect after a rich meal.

**INGREDIENTS**

*Serves 4*
4 apples
30ml/2 tbsp lemon juice
30ml/2 tbsp rose-water
45–60ml/3–4 tbsp icing sugar
crushed ice, to serve

--- COOK'S TIP ---

Pears are also excellent in this light refreshing dessert. Choose ripe pears if using them. They will yield when gently pressed at the stalk end, but take care not to bruise them.

*1* Carefully and thinly cut the peel from the apples using a swivel peeler. Discard the peel. Work quickly, otherwise the apples will begin to brown. If necessary, place the peeled apples in a bowl of lemony water while you peel the others.

*2* Grate the apples coarsely into a bowl, discarding the cores, then transfer to a pretty serving dish.

*3* Stir in the lemon juice, rose-water and add icing sugar to taste.

*4* Chill for at least 30 minutes and serve with crushed ice.

# Pineapple Ice Cream

**INGREDIENTS**

*Serves 8–10*
8 eggs, separated
115g/4oz/½ cup caster sugar
2.5ml/½ tsp vanilla essence
600ml/1 pint/2½ cups whipping cream
60ml/4 tbsp icing sugar
425g/15oz can pineapple chunks
75g/3oz/¾ cup pistachio nuts, chopped
wafer biscuits, to serve

*1* Place the egg yolks in a bowl, add the sugar and vanilla essence and beat until thick and pale.

*2* In a separate bowl, whip the cream and icing sugar to soft peaks, add to the egg yolk mixture and mix well.

*3* Whisk the egg whites in a separate large bowl until they are firm and hold stiff peaks. Gently fold the egg whites into the cream mixture and blend well.

*4* Cut the pineapple into very small pieces, add the pistachio nuts and stir into the cream mixture and mix well with a spoon.

*5* Pour the mixture into an ice cream container and place in the freezer for a few hours until it is set and firm, stirring it once or twice.

*6* Cut into thick slices and serve in a pretty glass dish decorated with wafer biscuits.

# Baklava

This is queen of all pastries with its exotic flavours and is usually served for the Persian New Year on 21st March, celebrating the first day of spring.

## INGREDIENTS

*Serves 6–8*
350g/12oz/3¾ cups ground
   pistachio nuts
150g/5oz/1¼ cups icing sugar
15ml/1 tbsp ground cardamom
150g/5oz/⅔ cup unsalted butter,
   melted
450g/1lb filo pastry

**For the syrup**
450g/1lb/2 cups granulated
   sugar
300ml/½ pint/1¼ cups water
30ml/2 tbsp rose-water

*1* First make the syrup: place the sugar and water in a saucepan, bring to the boil and then simmer for 10 minutes until syrupy. Stir in the rose-water and leave to cool.

*2* Mix together the nuts, icing sugar and cardamom. Preheat the oven to 160°C/325°F/Gas 3 and brush a large rectangular baking tin with a little melted butter.

*3* Taking one sheet of filo pastry at a time, and keeping the remainder covered with a damp cloth, brush with melted butter and lay on the bottom of the tin. Continue until you have six buttered layers in the tin. Spread half of the nut mixture over, pressing down with a spoon.

*4* Take another six sheets of filo pastry, brush with butter and lay over the nut mixture. Sprinkle over the remaining nuts and top with a final layer of six filo sheets brushed again with butter. Cut the pastry diagonally into small lozenge shapes using a sharp knife. Pour the remaining melted butter over the top.

*5* Bake for 20 minutes then increase the heat to 200°C/400°F/Gas 6 and bake for 15 minutes until light golden in colour and puffed.

*6* Remove from the oven and drizzle about three quarters of the syrup over the pastry, reserving the remainder for serving. Arrange the baklava lozenges on a large glass dish and serve with extra syrup.

# *Omm Ali*

Here's an Egyptian version of bread and butter pudding.

## INGREDIENTS

*Serves 4*

10–12 sheets filo pastry
600ml/1 pint/2½ cups milk
250ml/8fl oz/1 cup double cream
1 egg, beaten
30ml/2 tbsp rose-water
50g/2oz/½ cup each chopped
  pistachio nuts, almonds and hazelnuts
115g/4oz/⅔ cup raisins
15ml/1 tbsp ground cinnamon
single cream, to serve

*1* Preheat the oven to 160°C/325°F/
Gas 3. Bake the filo pastry, on a
baking sheet, for 15–20 minutes until
crisp. Remove from the oven and raise
the temperature to 200°C/400°F/Gas 6.

*2* Scald the milk and cream by
pouring into a pan and heating
very gently until hot but not boiling.
Slowly add the beaten egg and the
rose-water. Cook over a very low heat,
until the mixture begins to thicken,
stirring all the time.

*3* Crumble the pastry using your
hands and then spread in layers
with the nuts and raisins into the base
of a shallow baking dish.

*4* Pour the custard mixture over the
nut and pastry base and bake in the
oven for 20 minutes until golden.
Sprinkle with cinnamon and serve with
single cream.

# Café Glacé

## INGREDIENTS

*Serves 4–6*

30–45ml/2–3 tbsp instant dried coffee
475ml/16fl oz/2 cups water
15ml/1 tbsp sugar
600ml/1 pint/2½ cups milk
ice cubes and vanilla ice cream,
    to serve
4–6 chocolate flakes, to decorate
8–12 crisp ice cream biscuits,
    to serve

─── COOK'S TIP ───

You'll need to provide straws and long
spoons for eating this dessert. Adjust the
amount of coffee and sugar to suit your taste.

*1* Dissolve the coffee in 120ml/
4fl oz/½ cup of boiling water in a
small mixing bowl. Add the sugar and
stir well until it dissolves. Chill for at
least 2 hours. Mix together the milk
and water in a large jug. Add the
chilled coffee and stir well.

*2* Pour the coffee mixture into long
glasses until they are three quarters
full. Add ice cubes and the ice cream to
the top of each glass. Decorate with the
chocolate flakes and serve with the ice
cream biscuits.

# Sweet Pudding

This is a popular pudding in the
Arab countries. It has a smooth,
silky texture and a subtle flavour.

## INGREDIENTS

*Serves 4*

50g/2oz/¼ cup ground rice
45ml/3 tbsp cornflour
1.2 litres/2 pints/5 cups milk
75g/3oz/6 tbsp sugar
30ml/2 tbsp rose-water
50g/2oz/¾ cup ground almonds
25g/1oz/¼ cup ground pistachio nuts
ground cinnamon, to decorate
syrup or honey, melted, to serve

*1* Blend the ground rice and
cornflour to a paste with a little
cold milk in a small bowl.

*2* Bring the remaining milk to the
boil, add the sugar and simmer
gently. Gradually add the ground rice
paste to the milk, stirring constantly
with a wooden spoon to mix.

*3* Simmer the mixture on a very
gentle heat for 10–15 minutes,
until the mixture has thickened, stirring
frequently and being very careful not
to burn the bottom of the pan, which
would damage the very delicate flavour
of the rice.

*4* Stir in the rose-water and half of
the ground almonds and simmer
for a further 5 minutes.

*5* Cool for a few minutes and then
pour into a serving bowl or
individual dishes. Sprinkle with the
remaining ground almonds and the
pistachio nuts and decorate with a
dusting of ground cinnamon. Serve
with melted syrup or honey.

# Date and Nut Pastries

## INGREDIENTS

### Makes 35–40

450g/1lb/4 cups plain flour
225g/8oz/1 cup unsalted butter, cut into cubes
45ml/3 tbsp rose-water
60–75ml/4–5 tbsp milk
icing sugar, for sprinkling

### For the filling

225g/8oz/1¼ cups dates, stoned and chopped
175g/6oz/1¼ cups walnuts, finely chopped
115g/4oz/¾ cup blanched almonds, chopped
50g/2oz/½ cup pistachio nuts, chopped
120ml/4fl oz/½ cup water
115g/4oz/½ cup sugar
10ml/2 tsp ground cinnamon

1 Preheat the oven to 160°C/325°F/ Gas 3. First make the filling: place the dates, walnuts, almonds, pistachios, water, sugar and cinnamon in a small saucepan and cook over a low heat until the dates are soft and the water has been absorbed.

2 Place the flour in a large bowl and add the butter, working it into the flour with your fingertips.

3 Add the rose-water and milk and knead the dough until it's soft.

4 Take walnut-size lumps of dough. Roll each into a ball and hollow with your thumb. Pinch the sides.

5 Place a spoonful of date mixture in the hollow and then press the dough back over the filling to seal.

6 Arrange the pastries on a large baking tray. Press to flatten them slightly. Make little dents with a fork on the pastry. Bake in the oven for 20 minutes. Do not let them change colour or the pastry will become hard. Cool slightly and then sprinkle with icing sugar and serve.

# Yellow Rice Pudding

This baked rice pudding, *Sholezard*, is one of the most delicious desserts in all of Persia.

## INGREDIENTS

*Serves 6–8*

225g/8oz/1 cup short grain rice
1.5 litres/2½ pints/6¼ cups water
350g/12oz/1½ cups caster sugar
2–3 saffron strands, dissolved in 15ml/
 1 tbsp boiling water
60ml/4 tbsp rose-water
2.5ml/½ tsp ground cardamom
50g/2oz/¾ cup chopped blanched
 almonds
25g/1oz/2 tbsp butter
25g/1oz/¼ cup chopped pistachio nuts
5ml/1 tsp ground cinnamon

*1* Preheat the oven to 150°C/300°F/ Gas 2. Place the rice and water in a large pan, bring to the boil and simmer until the rice is soft and swollen.

*2* Pour 250ml/8fl oz/1 cup water into another saucepan, add the sugar and simmer for 10 minutes. Add the saffron, rose-water, cardamom and 25g/1oz/ ⅓ cup of the almonds. Stir well.

*3* Pour the syrup over the rice, add the butter and stir well.

---
COOK'S TIP
---

Make sure that the sugar is completely dissolved before the syrup begins to boil, then reduce the heat and simmer the syrup without stirring.

*4* Pour the rice mixture into an ovenproof dish, cover with a lid or with foil and bake in the oven for 30 minutes.

*5* Remove from the oven and decorate with the remaining almonds and pistachio nuts, dust with cinnamon and then chill before serving or serve warm.

# Almond Fingers

A very simple Middle Eastern sweetmeat which is especially popular in Arab countries, where it is known as Zeinab's Fingers.

## INGREDIENTS

*Makes 40–50*

200g/7oz/2¼ cups ground almonds
50g/2oz/½ cup ground pistachio nuts
50g/2oz/¼ cup granulated sugar
15ml/1 tbsp rose-water
2.5ml/½ tsp ground cinnamon
12 sheets of filo pastry
115g/4oz/½ cup melted butter
icing sugar, to decorate

*1* Preheat the oven to 160°C/325°F/ Gas 3. Mix together the almonds, pistachio nuts, sugar, rose-water and cinnamon for the filling.

*2* Cut each sheet of filo pastry into four rectangles. Work with one rectangle at a time, and cover the remaining rectangles with a damp dish towel to prevent them from drying.

*3* Brush one of the rectangles of filo pastry with a little melted butter and place a heaped teaspoon of the nut filling in the centre.

*4* Fold in the sides and roll into a finger or cigar shape. Continue making "cigars" until all the filling has been used.

*5* Place the fingers on a buttered baking sheet and bake in the oven for 30 minutes or until lightly golden.

*6* Remove and cool and then dust with icing sugar.

# Coconut Halva

This delicious coconut cake, traditionally called *Basbousa*, can be served either hot as a dessert or cold with tea.

## INGREDIENTS

*Serves 4–6*

115g/4oz/½ cup unsalted butter
175g/6oz/¾ cup sugar
50g/2oz/½ cup plain flour
150g/5oz/1¼ cups semolina
75g/3oz/1½ cups grated
  coconut
175ml/6fl oz/¾ cup milk
5ml/1 tsp baking powder
5ml/1 tsp vanilla essence
almonds, to decorate

**For the syrup**

115g/4oz/½ cup caster sugar
150ml/¼ pint/⅔ cup water
15ml/1 tbsp lemon juice

*1* First make the syrup, place the sugar, water and lemon juice in a saucepan, stir to mix and then bring to the boil and simmer for 6–8 minutes until the syrup has thickened. Allow to cool and chill.

*2* Preheat the oven to 180°C/350°F/ Gas 4. Melt the butter in a pan. Add the sugar, flour, semolina, coconut, milk, baking powder and vanilla and mix thoroughly.

*3* Pour the cake mixture into a shallow baking tin, flatten the top and bake in the oven for 30–35 minutes until the top is golden.

*4* Remove the halva from the oven and cut into diamond-shaped lozenges. Pour the cold syrup evenly over the top and decorate with an almond placed in the centre of each diamond-shaped piece.

# *Index*

# Lamb Koutlets

*Koutlets* are very tasty and are popular hot at a buffet or cold as snack or for picnics.

**INGREDIENTS**

*Makes 12–15*
3 eggs
1 onion, grated
30ml/2 tbsp chopped fresh
   parsley
450g/1lb new potatoes, peeled
450g/1lb finely minced lean lamb
115g/4oz/1 cup dried breadcrumbs
oil, for frying
salt and freshly ground black pepper
mint leaves, to garnish
pitta bread and herby green salad,
   to serve

*1* Beat the eggs in a large bowl, add the onion and parsley, season with salt and pepper and beat together.

*2* Cook the potatoes in a saucepan of boiling salted water for 20 minutes, until tender, then drain and leave to cool. When the potatoes are cold, grate them coarsely and stir into the egg mixture together with the minced lamb. Knead by hand for 3–4 minutes until thoroughly blended.

*3* Take a handful of meat and roll it into a ball. Roll the balls in the breadcrumbs and then mould them into triangles, about 13cm/5in long. Coat in the breadcrumbs again.

*4* Heat the oil in a frying pan and fry the *koutlets* over a medium heat for 8–12 minutes until golden brown, turning occasionally. Serve hot, garnished with mint and accompanied by pitta bread and salad.

---

# Dill and Broad Bean Meatballs

Here's another recipe for *kofta*, *Kofta Baghali*, this time using lean minced beef instead of the more common lamb.

**INGREDIENTS**

*Serves 4*
115g/4oz/½ cup long grain rice
450g/1lb minced lean beef
115g/4oz/1 cup plain flour
3 eggs, beaten
115g/4oz/1 cup broad beans,
   skinned
30ml/2 tbsp chopped fresh dill
25g/1oz/2 tbsp butter
   or margarine
1 large onion, chopped
2.5ml/½ tsp ground turmeric
1.2 litres/2 pints/5 cups water
salt and freshly ground black pepper
chopped fresh parsley, to garnish
naan bread, to serve

*1* Put the rice in a pan of water and boil for about 4 minutes until half cooked. Drain and place in a bowl with the meat, flour, eggs and seasoning. Knead thoroughly by hand until well blended.

*2* Add the skinned broad beans and dill and knead again thoroughly until the mixture is firm and pasty. Shape the mixture into large balls and set aside on a plate.

*3* Melt the butter or margarine in a large saucepan or flameproof casserole and fry the onion for 3–4 minutes until golden. Stir in the turmeric, cook for 30 seconds and then add the water and bring to the boil.

*4* Add the meatballs to the pan, reduce the heat and simmer for 45–60 minutes until the gravy is reduced to about 250ml/8fl oz/1 cup. Garnish with parsley and serve with naan bread.